W9-DDH-421

Conversation Strategies

Pair and Group Activities
for Developing
Communicative Competence

David Kehe
Peggy Dustin Kehe

with illustrations by Andrew Toos

PRO LINGUA ASSOCIATES

Published by Pro Lingua Associates
P. O. Box 1348
Brattleboro, Vermont 05302 USA

SAN 216-0579

802-257-7779
800-366-4775

*At Pro Lingua,
our objective is to foster
an approach to learning and teaching that
we call **Interplay**, the **inter**action of language
learners and teachers with their materials,
with the language and the culture, and
with each other in active, creative,
and productive **play**.*

ISBN 0-86647-082-4

This book was set in Century Schoolbook type by Stevens Graphics of Brattleboro, Vermont. It was printed and bound by Sheridan Books in Fredericksburg, Virginia.

Designed by Arthur A. Burrows

Printed in the United States of America
First edition. Fifth printing 2002
21,500 copies in print.

Introduction

This book is a collection of activities for pair/small group conversation practice. It is designed for use with a wide range of intermediate level students of English as a second or foreign language. The format of the activities puts the focus on the students, rather than the teacher. At the same time, the activities are designed to be nonthreatening to even the most reserved students. They are also enjoyable for both students and teachers, and they are easy for any teacher to implement.

A special feature of these activities is that they will develop strategic conversation skills. These are skills that go along with linguistic and sociolinguistic skills (grammar, vocabulary and usage). Strategic skills help the speaker/ listener keep a conversation going to its natural or desired conclusion. These skills include:

◇ beginning a conversation

◇ clarifying something

◇ interrupting someone

◇ rephrasing something

◇ correcting someone

◇ eliciting information

◇ soliciting attention

◇ repairing a conversation

◇ summarizing a conversation

◇ escaping from a conversation

◇ ending a conversation

The format of this book is quite simple. Each activity has three parts: a teacher's introduction, a student's introductory exercise, and pair/small group practice.

◇ The **teacher's introduction** is very short. It is located in the Appendix.

◇ The **introductory exercise** focuses on the words and expressions students need to carry out the activity. The students can do this individually and then check it with a partner.

◇ The **pair/small group practice** makes use of information-gap and other interactive formats.

It is not necessary to follow the order of the activities in this book. Each activity is complete and does not depend on another activity. However, Activity number 1, "Rejoinders," is a good place to begin, because the rejoinders can be used in virtually all of the other activities. So jump in and start talking, OK?

◇ *Acknowledgments* ◇

Our thanks to Berit Stevens and our other colleagues and students in language schools and colleges in Niger, Africa; Nagoya, Japan; Lesbos Island, Greece; and the U.S. who used these materials over the past 16 years and inspired us to put them into book form.

David Kehe
Peggy Dustin Kehe

Contents

◇ Rejoinders ◇

Happy
> **That's great!**
> **Terrific!**
> **Wonderful!**

Sad
> **That's too bad.**
> **I'm sorry to hear that.**
> **Oh, no!**

Interested
> **I see.**
> **That's nice.**
> **Oh, yeah?**

Surprised
> **You're kidding!**
> **I can't believe it!**
> **Oh, really! / Oh, really?**

See the teacher's introduction on page 106.

Introductory Exercise

Fill in the blanks with the phrases in **bold type**.

I see   That's great   That's too bad

1. A: Hi, how was the tennis match?

2. B: I won!

3. A: _____! Who did you play with?

4. B: My brother.

5. A: _____.

6. B: But after the game, he fell down and hurt his leg.

7. A: _____.

yeah   I see   That's nice

8. B: I just talked to my father on the phone.

9. A: Oh, _____?

10. B: He decided to go to Wisconsin instead of Florida for his vacation.

11. A: Oh, really? _____.

12. B: He said he's really busy at work these days.

13. A: _____.

I'm sorry to hear that   Wonderful   kidding

14. A: Guess what the doctor told me. I'm going to have a baby!

15. B: You're _____!

16. A: And he said I'm in good health.

17. B: _____!

18. A: And he said you should start doing some of the housework.

19. B: Oh, _____.

Terrific   Oh, no   can't believe it

20. A: We're having problems with the car again.

21. B: _____! What's the matter this time?

22. A: It won't start.

23. B: I _____! We just had it repaired last week.

24. A: I've got an idea. Let's get a new car.

25. B: _____!

Student A

Step 1. Say these sentences to Student B. Student B will respond with a rejoinder.

1. My friend broke her leg while skiing.
2. I have one brother and one sister.
3. My sister lost her purse again.
4. My father is a famous movie star.
5. A friend of mine was taken to the hospital last night.

Step 2. Listen to Student B and choose a correct rejoinder.

6. That's nice.
   Really?

7. That's great! (for you)
   I'm sorry to hear that. (because I'll miss you)

8. Terrific!
   I can't believe it!

9. You're kidding!
   Oh, yeah?

10. Really!
    I see.

Step 3. First fill in the blanks. Then say these sentences to Student B, who will respond with a rejoinder. Then listen to Student B and respond with a rejoinder.

1. I don't feel well today.
3. I heard there will be two days off from school next week.
5. I like _____ cars.
7. I'm going to play basketball in the next Olympics.
9. My brother is _____ .
11. We have a new teacher named Mr. Smith at our school.
13. I had a car accident, and the police took away my driver's license.
15. I have a date with _____ tonight.
17. Last night I drank five glasses of _____ in one hour.
19. Two days ago, I bought a pencil.

Step 4. Take turns with your partner. One person tells about a recent travel experience, and the other gives rejoinders.

Student B

Step 1. Listen to Student A and choose a correct rejoinder.

1. That's great!
   That's too bad.
2. That's nice.
   Oh, no!
3. I see.
   I can't believe it!
4. Sorry to hear that.
   Terrific!
5. Is that right?
   Oh, no!

Step 2. Say these sentences to Student A. Student A will respond
with a rejoinder.

6. My little brother likes fruit.
7. I'm going to Hawaii for two years.
8. My neighbor was arrested by the police this morning.
9. I think there was a ghost in my bedroom last night.
10. Somebody took my new jeans at the laundromat.

Step 3. First fill in the blanks. Then listen to Student A and respond
with a rejoinder. Then say these sentences to Student A, who
will respond with a rejoinder.

2. In elementary school, I was the best student in my class.
4. I caught a terrible cold last weekend.
6. I'm taking a trip to _____ on my next vacation.
8. The radio said that it's going to snow in _____
   tonight.
10. It takes me _____ minutes to get to school every day.
12. I have a pet dog and a pet _____ .
14. I would like to work in an office someday.
16. I drink _____ every day.
18. I am going to have a baby.
20. I'm going to buy a new notebook tomorrow.

Step 4. Take turns with your partner. One person tells about a recent
travel experience, and the other gives rejoinders.

◇ **Follow-Ups** ◇

What _____ ?   What kind of _____ ?

Where _____ ?   How long/far/late/big _____ ?

When _____ ?

See the teacher's introduction on page 106.

Introductory Exercise One

Fill in the blanks with the words or phrases in **bold type**.

Where   Oh, really   see   What

1. A: (*Question*) What time did you go to bed last night?

2. B:.   (*Answer*) At midnight.

3. A: (*Rejoinder & follow-up*) _____? That's late!

        _____ were you doing until midnight?

4. B: (*Answer*) I had a date.

5. A: (*Rejoinder & follow-up*) I _____.

        _____ did you go?

6. B: (*Answer*) We went to a party at a friend's house.

> **kidding   kind of   very hard   long**
> **How difficult   no   Really**

7. A: We have a test tomorrow.

8. B: _____ ? What _____ test?

9. A: It's on vocabulary.

10. B: Oh, _____ ! How _____ are you going to study for it?

11. A: Four or five hours.

12. B: You're _____ ! _____ are these vocabulary tests?

13. A: For me, they're _____ . I failed the last one.

Introductory Exercise Two

Think of answers, rejoinders, and follow-up questions, and write them in the following blanks.

14. A: (*Question*) What kind of job do you want in the future?

15. B: (*Answer*) _____ .

16. A: (*Rejoinder & follow-up*) _____ .

17. B: (*Answer*) _____ .

18. A: (*Rejoinder & follow-up*) _____ .

19. B: (*Answer*) _____ .

20. A: (*Question*) Do you have a roommate?

21. B: (*Answer*) _____ .

22. A: (*Rejoinder & follow-up*) _____ .

23. B: (*Answer*) _____ .

24. A: (*Rejoinder & follow-up*) _____ .

25. B: (*Answer*) _____ .

Student A

Step 1. Ask Student B these questions and respond with rejoinders and *several* follow-up questions. Also, answer Student B's questions.

1. What country would you like to visit someday?
3. How many members are there in your family?
5. Have you read any books or seen any movies lately?
7. Are you happy you're a student in this school?
9. Are you afraid of anything?
11. What did you do during the last vacation?
13. Do you have any problems in your life nowadays?
15. Do you like children?

Step 2. With a partner, write several questions in the space below.

Step 3. Find a new partner and take turns asking your questions and responding with rejoinders and follow-up questions.

Student B

Step 1. Ask Student A these questions and respond with rejoinders and *several* follow-up questions. Also, answer Student A's questions.

2. Did you watch TV last weekend?
4. Recently, what are you most worried about?
6. What were you doing a year ago?
8. What is your country's biggest problem today?
10. Do you like to exercise?
12. Who is the most unusual person in your family?
14. What would you like to do during your next vacation?
16. Would you like something to drink?

Step 2. With a partner, write several questions in the space below.

Step 3. Find a new partner and take turns asking your questions and responding with rejoinders and follow-up questions.

◇ **Confirmation Questions** ◇

How ____ ?   Which ____ ?   Is it ____ ?
Could you repeat that?

Vocabulary. Look at the shapes and fill in the blanks.

1. ○ c _____
2. ▢ s _____
3. ▭ r _____
4. ▷ t _____
5. — l _____
6. ∕∕ s _____   l _____
7. ﹏ w _____   l _____

↓ t _____

b _____

8. u _____   l _____   c _____
         l _____   r _____   c _____

See the teacher's introduction on page 107.

Correct answers are on page 10.

Introductory Exercise

Fill in the blanks with the words or phrases in **bold type** and then draw the shapes on another piece of paper. Then compare your drawing with a classmate's.

which corner   **How big**   **How many**   **Sure**
Is it   **Could you repeat that**   **got it**

1. A: In the middle of the paper, there's a circle, about 2 centimeters across.

2. B: _____ centimeters?

3. A: Two. In the upper right corner of the paper, there's a triangle, about 2 centimeters on each side.

4. B: In _____ ?

5. A: In the upper right corner. Then there's a line going from the lower left corner of the triangle to the top of the circle.

6. B: _____ a straight line?

7. A: Yeah, a straight one. In the upper left corner of the paper, there's a rectangle, 4 across and 2 up and down.

8. B: _____ , please?

9. A: _____ . In the upper left corner of the paper, there's a rectangle. This rectangle is about 4 centimeters by 2 centimeters.

10. B: OK, I've _____ .

11. A: In the lower left corner of the paper, there's a square, 2 by 2 centimeters.

12. B: _____ ?

13. A: About 2 by 2. Finally, inside this square, there's a wavy line which goes from the lower left to the upper right. And that's all.

Answers to vocabulary: 1. circle; *2.* square; *3.* rectangle; *4.* triangle; *5.* line; *6.* straight line *or* slanted line; *7.* wavy line; *8.* top, bottom, upper left corner, lower right corner.

Student A

Step 1. Describe this design to Student B. Student B will draw it.

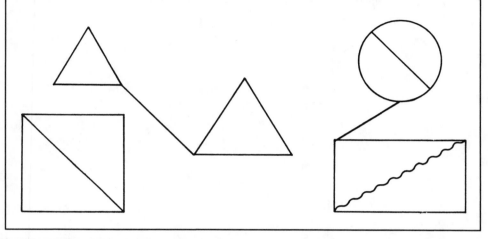

Step 2. Listen to Student B. Draw the design.

Step 3. Draw a design of your own. Find a new partner and take turns describing and drawing the designs.

Student B

Step 1. Listen to Student A. Draw the design.

Step 2. Describe this design to Student A. Student A will draw it.

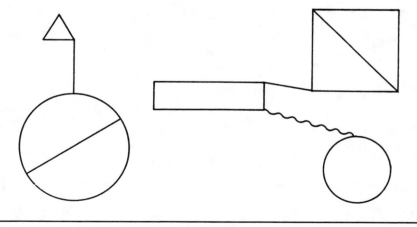

Step 3. Draw a design of your own. Find a new partner and take turns describing and drawing the designs.

── ◇ Clarifications ◇ ──
with Question Words

Excuse me.
Sorry.
Pardon (me)?
}
You did *what* ?
He went *where* ?
She's coming *when* ?
He's *how old* ?
Who will we meet ?
We'll meet *who* ?
Who will meet us?
I didn't understand *what* you said .
What did you say ?

See the teacher's introduction on page 107.

Introductory Exercise

Fill in the blanks with the words or phrases in **bold type**.

I see   **Sorry**   **before** *what*   **Excuse**   **carries a** *what*

1. A: My father carries a *blah blah* when he visits a foreign country.

2. B: _____ me. He _____ ?

3. A: A dictionary.

4. B: Oh, a dictionary. _____ .

5. A: Before *blah blah*, I always take a bath.

6. B: _____ . You take a bath _____ ?

7. A: Before dinner.

8. B: I see.

Who will take   didn't understand   *What* did you
speak *what*   *Who* will we meet   OK

9. A: If you see *blah blah*, tell him *blah blah*.

10. B: Excuse me. _____ say ?

11. A: If you see Bill, tell him I need his help.

12. B: _____ .

13. A: I know how to speak *blah blah* very well.

14. B: Sorry. You _____ very well?

15. A: Spanish.

16. B: I see.

17. A: When you arrive at the university, a student advisor will take you to your dorm.

18. B: Pardon? _____ us ?

19. A: A student advisor. Then you'll meet with the dorm supervisor.

20. B: Excuse me. I _____ . _____ ?

21. A: The dorm supervisor. He's in charge of the dorm.

Student A

Step 1. Say these sentences to Student B. Clarify your sentence when
Student B asks you to.

1. I'm planning to go to *blah blah* on my next vacation.
2. I need to buy a *blah blah*.
3. Blah blah is very *blah blah*.
4. It costs *blah blah* to buy new shoes.
5. *Blah blah* told us to stay here.
6. After I finish my homework, I watch *blah blah*.

Step 2. Listen to Student B. *Choose* one of the clarifying sentences and
ask Student B to clarify their sentence.

7. Sorry. His *what* is old?
   Sorry. *When* did he go?

8. Excuse me. *Who* must arrive?
   Excuse me. Before *when*?

9. Sorry. *Who* do you want?
   Sorry. I didn't understand what you said.

10. Pardon? She's *how many* years old?
    Pardon? *Why* did she do that?

11. Sorry. You have to do *what*?
    Sorry. *Who* did you talk to?

Step 3. Say these sentences to Student B. Then clarify them.
Then ask your partner to clarify their sentences.

1. After you *blah blah*, I want you to help me.
3. *Blah blah* is my favorite sport.
5. It usually costs about *blah blah* to buy a movie ticket in my country.
7. If you *blah blah*, don't forget to *blah blah*.
9. When I arrived at the meeting, there were only about *blah blah*
   people there.

Student B

Step 1. Listen to Student A. *Choose* one of the clarifying sentences and ask Student A to clarify their sentence.

1. Excuse me. You're eating *what*?
   Excuse me. You're going *where*?

2. Pardon? You need to see a *what*?
   Pardon? You need to buy a *what*?

3. Sorry. What did you say?
   Sorry. You did *what*?

4. Sorry. You will go *where*?
   Sorry. It costs *how much*?

5. Excuse me. *Who* told us?
   Excuse me. She told us to stay *where*?

6. Pardon? You watch *what*?
   Pardon? You went *where*?

Step 2. Say these sentences to Student A. Clarify your sentence when Student A asks you to.

7. His *blah blah* is very old.
8. We must arrive before *blah blah*.
9. I want you to *blah blah* and *blah blah*.
10. My sister had a birthday party yesterday. She's *blah blah* years old.
11. If you see the teacher, tell her that I have to *blah blah* so I can't come to school.

Step 3. Ask Student A to clarify their sentences. Then ask Student A these sentences and clarify them.

2. I always eat *blah blah* for lunch.
4. I think you look like *blah blah*.
6. My best friend told me to *blah blah*.
8. *Blah blah* gave me some medicine because I was starting to feel sick.
10. Do you know what car I like best? I love *blah blah*.

— ◇ **Keeping or Killing** ◇ — the Conversation

Killers	*Keepers*
I don't really know.	**What do you think?**
That's a good question.	**How do you feel?**
I'm not sure.	**How about you?**
I have no idea.	**What about you?**
I'd have to think about that.	
Umm, ahhh, I'd rather not say.	

See the teacher's introduction on page 108.

Introductory Exercise

Use words from the *killers* and *keepers* phrases in the box above and fill in the blanks.

1.   *How to **kill** the conversation when you don't know what to say:*

   A: What are you planning to do next weekend?

   B: I don't _____ know.

2.   *How to **keep** the conversation going when you don't know what to say:*

   A: What are you planning to do next weekend?

   B: I'm not _____ . What about _____ ?

   A: I'm thinking of going to the beach.

3.   *How to **kill** the conversation when you are asked an embarrassing question:*

   A: How old are you?

   B: Umm, ahhh. I'd ———————————————— not say.

4.   *How to **keep** the conversation going when you are asked an embarrassing question:*

   A: How old are you?

   B: That's a good ——————————— . How ——————————— you?

   A: I'm 26. But I think you're younger than I am.

5.   *How to **kill** the conversation when the question is difficult:*

   A: Don't you think there are too many problems with nuclear power?

   B: I have ———————————————— idea.

6.   *How to **keep** conversation going when the question is difficult:*

   A: Don't you think there are too many problems with nuclear power?

   B: I would have to ——————————— . ——————————— do you think?

   A: I think it is dangerous and expensive, and I . . . .

7.   *How to **kill** the conversation when you don't want to answer.*

   A: How do you feel about our teacher ?

   B: Umm, uhh, I'd rather ———————————————————— .

8.   *How to **keep** the conversation, even if you don't want to answer .*

   A: How do you feel about our teacher?

   B: That's a good ——————————— . How ——————————————— ?

Student A

Step 1. Ask your partner these questions. Also, listen to your partner's questions, but do not answer them, and use the "killers and keepers" to respond.

1. What's the best age to get married?
3. What are you going to do during the next vacation?
5. Don't you think being an airplane pilot would be a great job?
7. Who do you think is the greatest writer in the world?
9. Which city is the most beautiful in the world?
11. Who is your favorite singer?
13. What is the best sport for staying healthy?
15. What do you like to drink at parties?

Step 2. With your partner, write some new questions in the space below. A few questions can be embarrassing, and a few difficult.

Step 3. Find a new partner, read your questions, and use the "killers and keepers" to respond to your partner's questions.

Student B

Step 1. Ask your partner these questions. Also, listen to your partner's questions, but do not answer them, and use the "killers and keepers" to respond.

2. Do you think there will be a big war soon?
4. How many children should a married couple have?
6. How much do you weigh? (What's your weight?)
8. Don't you wish you were in elementary school again?
10. What's a good way to improve our English?
12. What type of job do you want to have in the future?
14. What's the biggest problem in the world today?

Step 2. With your partner, write some new questions in the space below. A few questions can be embarrassing, and a few difficult.

Step 3. Find a new partner, read your questions, and use the "killers and keepers" to respond to your partner's questions.

◊ **Probability Expressions** ◊

100%	**sure** **definitely**	**will**
75%	**probably** **(there's) a good chance**	**should** **ought to**
50%	**not sure** **don't know**	**might** **may** **could**
25%	**don't think (so)** **probably not/won't** **doubt (that)**	**shouldn't** **ought not to**
0%	**no chance** **definitely not** **No way!**	**won't**

See the teacher's introduction on page 108.

Introductory Exercises

Fill in the blanks with the words or phrases in **bold type**.

There's a good chance we will.   There might be.
don't think   sure I won't   They'll definitely have some.

1. A: Do you think your aunt will visit us next month?

2. B: *(25%)*: No, I _____ she'll come.

3. A: We need some tomatoes. Do you think the store will have some today?

4. B: *(100%)*: _____ .

5. A: I wonder if there will be a movie on TV tonight.

6. B: *(50%)*: _____ .

7. A: Be careful at work today. There are a lot of people with colds these days.

8. B: *(0%)*: Don't worry. I'm _____ get sick.

9. A: Do you think we'll have time to eat dinner before the concert starts?

10. B: *(75%)*: _____ .

No chance   probably   I doubt it   way

11. A: You'd better be careful. Someone might steal your car.

12. B: *(0%)*: No _____ . I have a special lock on it.

13. A: You don't look well. Are you getting a cold?

14. B: *(75%)*: I _____ am. My sister has one now, too.

15. A: Do you think you'll run a marathon this year ?

16. B: *(0%)*: _____ . I can't even run 3 miles.

17. A: Do you think you'll go swimming this afternoon ?

18. B: *(25%)*: _____ . I heard it's supposed to rain this afternoon.

Student A

Step 1. First fill in the blanks. Then ask your partner these questions. Also, answer your partner's questions using "probability expressions." Try to explain your reasons with some details.

1. Do you think you'll visit _____ this year?

3. Do you think you'll have a _____ someday?

5. Do you think you'll go to bed after midnight tonight?

7. Do you think you'll live in _____ for the rest of your life?

9. Do you think you'll go _____ this month?

11. Do you think I'll pass this course?

13. Do you think you'll _____ within the next 5 days?

15. Do you think you'll eat _____ this weekend?

Step 2. With your partner, write some "probability questions" in the space below.

Step 3. Find a new partner and ask your questions. Also, answer your new partner's questions using the "probability expressions."

Student B

Step 1. First fill in the blanks. Then ask your partner these questions. Also answer your partner's questions using the "probability expressions." Try to explain your reasons with some details.

2. Do you think you'll eat _____ for dinner tonight?

4. Do you think you'll _____ for your next vacation?

6. Do you think you'll buy _____ this year?

8. Do you think you'll talk on the phone before tomorrow night?

10. Do you think I'll be rich someday?

12. Do you think you'll go _____ within the next 2 months?

14. Do you think you'll _____ soon?

16. Do you think I'll _____ soon?

Step 2. With your partner, write some "probability questions" in the space below.

Step 3. Find a new partner and ask your questions. Also, answer your new partner's questions using the "probability expressions."

◇ **Interruptions** ◇

Excuse me. *(polite)* **Wait a minute.** *(familiar or strong)*	**Could I say something?** **Can I say one thing?** **Can I ask something?** **But ___ .**

See the teacher's introduction on page 109.

Introductory Exercise

Fill in the blanks with the words or phrases in **bold type**.

yeah   great   Can I ask something
wondering   one thing   Excuse   ahead   Wait

1. A: I've got to tell you about my date last night.
2. B: Oh, yeah, I was _____ how it went.
3. A: It was _____. First we went out for pizza, and . . .
4. C: _____ me. _____?
    Who did you go out with?
5. A: Do you know Jean?
6. C: Oh, _____ .
7. A: As I was saying, after eating dinner, we went to the movie. I hate love stories, but that one was great. Then we went out for coffee after that, and . . .
8. B: Can I say _____?
9. A: Sure, go _____ .
10. B: I think you should have gone to Mike's party after the movie. Everyone was there.
11. A: Really? I didn't know about it. How was it?
12. C: _____ a minute. I told you about the party two days ago.

Student A

Step 1. With two partners, follow the instructions.

1. You start. Ask Student B: "How do you get to your house from here? Please tell me details."

2. Interrupt Student C. Say: "Excuse me. Can I say something? When I'm nervous, I _____ in order to feel calm."

3. You start. Ask Student B: "What were you doing last year at this time? Please give me a lot of details."

4. Answer Student C.

5. Interrupt Student C with a statement.

6. You start. Ask Student B: "What are your future plans? Please give me a lot of details."

7. Answer Student C.

8. Interrupt Student C with a question.

9. You start. Ask Student B: "What are the details of your favorite book or movie?"

10. Answer Student C.

Step 2. Choose a topic. Tell your partner about it. Also listen to your partners and interrupt them.

◆ Tell about a time when someone was angry with you.

◆ Tell about a time you won a prize or sporting event.

◆ Tell about what you did yesterday from noon to midnight.

◆ Other

Student B

Step 1. With two partners, follow the instructions.

1. Answer Student A.
2. You start. Ask Student C: "Can you tell me about a time when you were very nervous?"
3. Answer Student A.
4. Interrupt Student A with a question.
5. You start. Say to Student C: "Explain in detail how you study for English class."
6. Answer Student A.
7. Interrupt Student A with a statement.
8. You start. Say to Student C: "Tell me in detail what you do during your free time."
9. Answer Student A.
10. Interrupt Student A.

Step 2. Choose a topic. Tell your partner about it. Also listen to your partners and interrupt them.

◆ Tell about a time when someone was angry with you.

◆ Tell about a time you won a prize or sporting event.

◆ Tell about what you did yesterday from noon to midnight.

◆ Other

Student C

Step 1. With two partners, follow the instructions.

1 Interrupt Student B and say: "Excuse me. Can I ask you something? How many years have you lived in your house?"

2. Answer Student B.

3. Interrupt Student B. Say: "Excuse me. Can I say one thing? I think your life is better today because _____ ."

4. You start. Ask Student A: "Can you tell me about your favorite vacation in detail?"

5. Answer Student B.

6. Interrupt Student B with a statement.

7. You start. Say to Student A: "Talk about a problem you have now or had in the past."

8. Answer Student B.

9. Interrupt Student B with a question.

10. You start. Tell Student A: "Tell me about your family."

Step 2. Choose a topic. Tell your partner about it. Also listen to your partners and interrupt them.

◆ Tell about a time when someone was angry with you.

◆ Tell about a time you won a prize or sporting event.

◆ Tell about what you did yesterday from noon to midnight.

◆ Other

◊ Echoes ◊

Did you say ___?   You said ___?
That's ___ (, is it)?

Vocabulary. Look at the map and fill in the blanks.

1. The place where two streets meet is called an i_____ .

2.
       n_____

w_____   ✳   e_____

      s_____

3. The bank is a_____ the street from the shoe store.

4. The gas station is n_____ to the shoe store.

5. The gas station is b_____ the school and the shoe store.

6. The bank and the shoe store are on the c_____s.

7. The bank is on the n_____ side of Third Avenue.

See the teacher's introduction on page 109.

Correct answers are on page 30.

Introductory Exercise

Fill in the blanks with the words or phrases in **bold type**.

That's   At the top?
Did you   didn't you   You

1. A: We'll start by finding the coffee shop.

2. B: _____ say the coffee shop?

3. A: That's right. Do you see Kennedy Street at the top?

4. B: _____ ?

5. A: Yes, the top. Can you see Sunshine Avenue?

6. B: _____ said Sunshine?

7. A: Yes, on the right side.

8. B: ____ the right side, right?

9. A: Yes. OK. Where Kennedy and Sunshine meet is the coffee shop.

10. B: In the corner?

11. A: You said "on the corner," _____ ?

12. B: Right. It's "on the corner."

corner is it   I'm ready   You said
Which avenue   The west side   That's

13. A: Next, I'll tell you how to find the electronics shop.

14. B: OK, _____ .

15. A: Can you see Hawaii Avenue?

16. B: _____ ?

17. A: Hawaii.

18. B: _____ Hawaii?

19. A: Yes. And Star Street. It's at the bottom. At the intersection of Hawaii and Star is the electronics shop.

20. B: _____ at the intersection of Hawaii and Star, right?

21. A: Yes, the electronics shop is at the intersection of Hawaii and Star.

22. B: OK, which _____ ?

23. A: The corner on the west side.

24. B: _____ ?

25. A: Yes, the west side.

Answers: intersection, north, east, south, west, across, next, between, corner, north.

Student A

Step 1. Tell Student B how to find these places. Begin with *one, two,* etc.

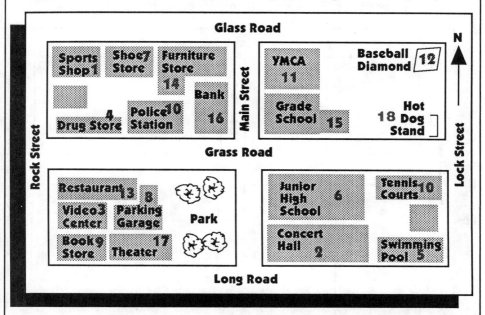

Step 2. Student B will tell you the location of some places. Echo these instructions. Then write the names on your map.

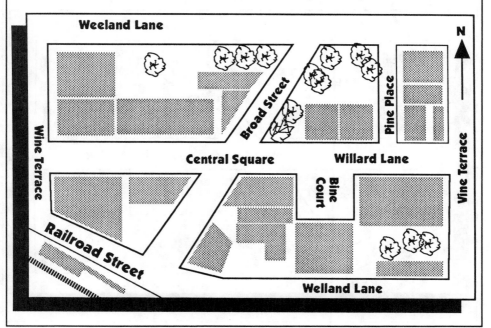

Student B

Step 1. Student A will tell you the location of some places. Echo these instructions. Then write the names on your map.

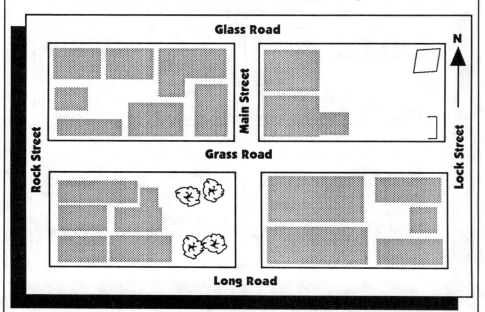

Step 2. Tell Student A how to find these places. Begin with *one, two,* etc.

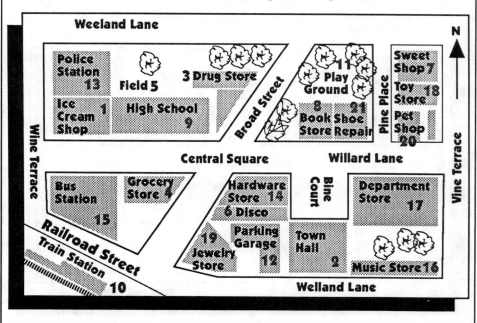

I SAY, OLD CHAP WOULD YOU MIND REMOVING YOUR SUB FROM MY SOUP?

◊ Polite Requests, ◊
Responses, and Excuses

Requests

Informal: *when you are speaking to friends, your family members, waiters, salespeople*

Would you lend me your pen?
Could I borrow your pen?

Formal: *when you are speaking to teachers, police, strangers, your boss, elderly people, important people*

Would you mind lending me your pen?
I wonder if I could borrow your pen.
Would you mind if I borrowed your pen?

Responses

Acceptance	*Refusal with an excuse*
Sure.	**I'm sorry, but I can't.**
I'd be glad to.	**I'm sorry, but ___ .**
All right.	**I'd like to, but ___ .**

See the teacher's introduction on page 110.

Introductory Exercise

Fill in the blanks with the words or phrases in **bold type**.

Would you mind   Could you   Sure   I'd like to, but

At home

1. *Brother*: _____ drive me to the train station at 5 o'clock?

2. *Sister*: _____ I'm leaving at 4 o'clock so I can't.

3. *Brother*: Thanks anyway. I'll ask somebody else.

On the street

4. *Young woman*: Excuse me. _____ telling me which way the tourist office is?

5. *Elderly man*: _____ . It's over there.

6. *Young woman*: Thank you.

Could you   Would you mind if   Sure   I'm sorry, but

At a store

7. *Customer*: _____ tell me how much this jacket costs?

8. *Salesperson*: _____ . It's $75.

9. *Customer*: Thanks.

At school

10. *Student*: _____ I visited your office tomorrow to show you my paper?

11. *Teacher*: _____ I'll be out of town tomorrow.

12. *Student*: I see. Thanks anyway.

All right   Could you wait   be glad to
I wonder if   Would you put

At work

13. *Worker*: _____ I could go out for lunch now.

14. *Boss*: _____ a half hour more?

15. *Worker*: _____ .

At a store

16. *Customer*: _____ this in a box for me, please?

17. *Salesperson*: Sure. I'd _____ .

Student A

Step 1. Say your sentences to Student B. Then listen to Student B.

1. Tell your partner, "I'm a police officer." Listen to your partner's request. Then **refuse** to help. **Give an excuse**.
2. Tell your partner, "I'm your mother." Listen to the request and **agree** to help.
3. Say, "I'm the head of the school." Listen and **refuse**. **Give an excuse**.
4. Say, "I'm a child." Listen and **agree**.

Step 2. First listen to Student B. Then make your request.

5. Ask your partner to weigh your package.
6. Ask your partner to lend you their umbrella.
7. Ask your partner to tell you where the drug store is.
8. Ask your partner to push your car. (Your car has broken down in the middle of the street.)

Step 3. Now you start again.

9. Say, "I'm the school secretary." Listen and **refuse**. **Give an excuse**.
10. Say, "I'm your boss." Listen and **refuse**. **Give an excuse**.
11. Say, "I'm a salesperson in a store." Listen and **agree**.
12. Say, "I'm your brother." Listen and **refuse**. **Give an excuse**.

Step 4. Now Student B will start again.

13. Ask your partner to tell you how much their car cost.
14. Ask your partner to lend you $75 so that you can go to a rock concert.
15. Ask your partner to lend you their car so you can travel for a week.
16. Ask your partner to pick you up at the station tonight at midnight.

Student B

Step 1. First listen to Student A. Then make your request.

1. Ask your partner to tell you where the nearest bus stop is.
2. Ask your partner to open the window.
3. Ask your partner to lend you a pencil.
4. Ask your partner if you could sit next to them.

Step 2. Say your sentences to Student A. Then listen to Student A.

5. Tell your partner, "I'm a post office worker." Listen and **agree** to help.
6. Say, "I'm your friend." Listen and **refuse. Give an excuse.**
7. Say, "I'm a middle-aged stranger." Listen and **refuse. Give an excuse.**
8. Say, "I'm a policeman." Listen and **refuse. Give an excuse.**

Step 3. Now Student A will start again.

9. Ask your partner if you could use the telephone on their desk.
10. Ask your partner to give you 3 days off from work. (You are tired and you need a rest.)
11. Ask your partner to tell you where the restroom is.
12. Ask your partner to help you with your homework at 9 o'clock tonight.

Step 4. Now you start again.

13. Say, "I'm your future father-in-law." Listen and **agree.**
14. Say, "I'm your boss." Listen and **refuse. Give an excuse.**
15. Say, "I'm your sister." Listen and **refuse. Give an excuse.**
16. Say, "I'm your father." Listen and **agree.**

See the teacher's introduction on page 110.

◇ **Response Questions** ◇

What do you think?
How do you feel about that?
Don't you agree?
Do you know what I mean?

Introductory Exercise

Fill in the blanks with the words or phrases in **bold type.**

do you feel about that   Right   know what I mean

1. A: What gift do you think we should get our teacher?

2. B: I was thinking about some jewelry. How _____ ?

3. A: That's a good idea, but I'm not sure what her taste is.
   Do you _____ ?

4. B: You mean, for example, she might prefer silver rather than gold?

5. A: _____ . Or she might not like large earrings.

How do you feel   you agree   That's a good idea

6. B: How about money? We could collect some and give it to her. Everyone
   likes money. Don't _____ ?

7. A: Yes, but it seems kind of cold. How about a gift certificate? She could
   buy something she likes. _____ about that?

8. B: _____ .

Don't you agree   That's a good point
Do you know what I

9. A: Our school director asked me to recommend some improvements for our school. Do you have any ideas?

10. B: Sure. I think 8 a.m. is too early to start. _____ ?

11. A: Yes, but if we start later, it means we'll have to have afternoon classes. _____ mean?

12. B: _____ .

you know what I mean   a great idea
How do you feel about that

13. A: One thing that would improve the school would be to have more clubs. _____ ?

14. B: That's _____ . Then we could meet new people. Do _____ ?

15. A Yeah, that's true.

Student A

Step 1. Say line 1. Student B will choose a response and say it. Then you respond with a. or b. from 3, etc.

1. Could you help me choose a topic for my speech?
3. a. No. I don't have a job. Could you help me find one?
   b. No. My childhood was boring. I need something exciting.
5. a. That's a good point. But I'm not a funny person. Do you know what I mean?
   b. I don't agree. It's much too cold to go swimming. What do you think?

  ◆   ◆   ◆   ◆   ◆   ◆   ◆   ◆

2. a. We could watch TV. How do you feel about that?
   b. We should go to a dentist once a year. How do you feel about that?
4. a. I agree. TV is exciting. What do you think?
   b. Yeah, but it's cheap. Or we could take a walk in the park. What do you think?
6. a. Don't you think work is exciting?
   b. Okay, let's go to a concert. That's exciting.

Step 2. Get in groups of 3 to 4 students. Student A is the first "score keeper" for 8 minutes. The score keeper will:
   a. choose one of the topics for the discussion on Student B's page.
   b. tell the members when 8 minutes is finished.
   c. mark each time a group member uses one of the expressions on the score sheet.
The score keeper will **not** join in the discussion.

SCORE SHEET			
Expressions	**Student A**	**Student B**	**Student C**	**Student D**
What do you think?				
How do you feel about that?				
Don't you agree?				
Do you know what I mean?				

Steps 3, 4, 5, and 6 are at the bottom of Student B's page.

Student B

Step 1. Listen to Student A say line 1. You choose the best answer from line 2 and say it. Then student A will respond.

2. a. Sure. You can eat at my house. How do you feel about that?
   b. Sure. You could give a speech about your childhood. How do you feel about that?
4. a. How about something funny about you? Everyone enjoys funny stories. Don't you agree?
   b. How about basketball? We could go to a game this weekend.
6. a. Yes, you are! You'd be a great teacher.
   b. Yes, you are! You're always doing something funny.

◆   ◆   ◆   ◆   ◆   ◆   ◆   ◆

1.   What should we do tonight?
3. a. We watched TV last night. It's getting boring. Do you know what I mean?
   b. I feel sick. Do you know what I mean?
5. a. We should park the car. Don't you agree?
   b. We should do something more exciting than walking. Don't you agree?

Step 2. Student A has the directions. You have the topics.

DISCUSSION TOPICS

◆ You are opening a new international restaurant. Plan the menu.
◆ Plan a one-week trip. You have $500 to spend (per person).
◆ Make nicknames or English names for each student in this class. Explain your reasons.
◆ Make a list of the most important characteristics of a husband or a wife. Put the most important first, etc.
◆ Plan an interesting activity to do together this weekend.
◆ Make a list of the characteristics of a good teacher. Put the most important first, etc.
◆ Plan a new culture. Decide 10 customs this culture should have.

Step 3. Student B is the score keeper for 8 minutes.
Step 4. Student C is the score keeper for 8 minutes.
Step 5: If you have 4 members, Student D is the score keeper for 8 minutes.
Step 6: Get in new groups with different partners and explain some of the decisions you made during your discussions.

◇ **Solicitors** ◇

What do you mean ___ ?
Can you give me an example ___ ?
Could you tell me ___ ?
I'd be interested to know ___ .
I'd like to know ___ .
You said ___ . What did you mean?
Could you explain ___ ?
What kind of ___ ?

See the teacher's introduction on page 111.

Introductory Exercise

Fill in the blanks with the words or phrases in **bold type**.

What do you   Could you tell me

You said you   Could you give me   happened

1. A: My brother had a car accident.
2. B: Really? What _____ ?
3. A: Well, he was late for work and was driving fast.
4. B: _____ mean by "fast"?
5. A: About 10 miles over the speed limit.

◆   ◆   ◆   ◆   ◆   ◆   ◆   ◆   ◆

6. A: I had a great time during my trip to Hawaii.
7. B: _____ had a great time. _____ what you did there?
8. A: I played a lot of sports.
9. B: What kind of sports? _____ an example?
10. A: Tennis, swimming, volleyball, and surfing.

What kind   a little more about   What kind of

why   Could you explain   I'd be

11. A: I just bought a new car.
12. B: Great! _____?
13. A: A Ford.
14. B: _____ interested to know _____ you chose a Ford.
15. A: It had a good price and a nice color. Also, I liked the salesperson.

◆ ◆ ◆ ◆ ◆ ◆ ◆ ◆ ◆

16. A: I really like fishing.
17. B: Oh? _____ fishing ?
18. A. Trout fishing.
19. B: Could you tell me _____ trout fishing?
20. A: Well, first there's fly fishing.
21. B: _____ what that means ?
22. A: OK. The hook looks like a fly, and the trout tries to eat it, and then . . .

Student A

Step 1. First fill in the blanks. Then say the sentences to Student B and answer Student B's questions.

1. I want to have several children someday.
2. When I was younger, I was very bad.
3. In high school, my favorite subject was _____ .
4. In the future, I'd like to work as a _____ .

Step 2. Listen to Student B's statement. Then decide how to complete the question and ask it in order to get more details.

5. Could you tell me _____ ?
6. What do you mean _____ ?
7. Can you give me an example of _____ ?
8. You said _____ is _____ ? $\begin{cases} \text{What do you mean?} \\ \text{Why is it _____ ?} \end{cases}$

Step 3. Fill in the blanks and read these sentences to Student B. Also, answer Student B's questions.

9. I think pets are _____ .
10. _____ has the best food.
    (country name)
11. Single life is $\begin{cases} \text{better} \\ \text{worse} \end{cases}$ than married life.
12. I enjoy going out for dinner.
13. Having a car $\begin{cases} \text{is} \\ \text{isn't} \end{cases}$ important in my country.
14. _____ is my favorite _____ .

Step 4. Listen to Student B. Then ask several questions in order to get more details. Use the "solicitors."

Student B

Step 1. Listen to Student A's statement. Then decide how to complete the question and ask it in order to get more details.

1. What do you mean _____ ?
2. Can you give me an example _____ ?
3. Could you tell me _____ ?
4. You said you'd like to work as a _____ .

Could you tell me $\begin{cases} \text{what kind?} \\ \text{why?} \end{cases}$

Step 2. First fill in the blanks. Then say the sentences to Student A and answer Student A's questions.

5. My favorite holiday is _____ .
6. I think this is a funny class.
7. I like to watch TV.
8. I think living in the city is _____ than living in the countryside.

Step 3. Listen to Student A. Then ask several questions in order to get more details. Use the "solicitors."

Step 4. Fill in the blanks and say these sentences to Student A. Also, answer Student A's questions.

15. _____ makes me angry.

16. I prefer to spend time $\begin{cases} \text{alone.} \\ \text{with a lot of people.} \end{cases}$

17. Drinking alcohol $\begin{cases} \text{is} \\ \text{isn't} \end{cases}$ a problem in my country.

18. Money $\begin{cases} \text{is} \\ \text{isn't} \end{cases}$ important to me.

19. _____ is my favorite _____ .

◇ **Comparison Words** ◇

different/difference	**exactly**
the same	**rather**
identical	**somewhat**
similar	**slightly**
alike	**What else?**
opposite	

See the teacher's introduction on page 111.

Introductory Exercise

Fill in the blanks with the words or phrases in **bold type.**

How about you   Really   What else
one difference   identical

1. A: Let's start. You look at only picture B. I'll look at only picture A. What's in your picture?

2. B: I have a house. _____ ?

3. A: Yeah. I have one, too, in picture A.

4. B: _____ do you have?

5. A: There's a tree in mine.

6. B: _____ ? There's no tree in mine.

7. A: So that's _____ .

8. B: Right. Our pictures aren't _____ .

different   Yeah   Did you say
exactly opposite   Don't you

8. B: I have a car on a road.
9. A: _____ "a car"?
10. B: Yes. _____ have a car?
11. A: No. So that's _____ . Is there a hill in your picture?
12. B: _____ . Which side is your hill on?
13. A: On the right.
14. B: Really? Mine is on the left, so they're _____ .

similar   slightly
very   seem alike   somewhat the same

15. A: It's difficult to find differences, because the pictures _____ .
    They're just _____ different.
16. B: I don't agree. I'd say they're _____ different. They are
    not _____ at all.
17. A: But they are _____ . They both have a house, a hill, and
    a road.

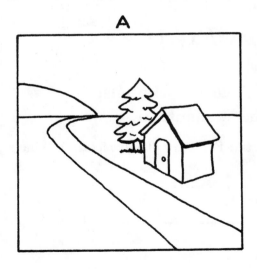

Student A

Look at your picture. Student B's picture is different. Talk about your pictures and find the differences.

fence	truck	car	pine tree	curved
cloud	smoke	chimney	curtain	grass
walk	upstairs	steps	flower	(on a) leash
yard	garage	shade tree	straight	downstairs

Student B

Look at your picture. Student A's picture is different. Talk about your pictures and find the differences.

fence	truck	car	pine tree	curved
cloud	smoke	chimney	curtain	grass
walk	upstairs	steps	flower	(on a) leash
yard	garage	shade tree	straight	downstairs

◇ Word Finders ◇

The word I'm looking for	**thing**
What do you/we call __ ?	**gadget**
What's it (called) ?	**whachamacallit**
It's used for __ .	**thingamajig**
You see it __ .	
It looks like __ .	

See the teacher's introduction on page 112.

Introductory Exercise One

Read the description and tell what it is. (The answers are on the next page.)

A.   This is something we read. Most people get one every day. In it, we can read about the news, sports, and entertainment. It also has some pictures. It's black and white, but it's read everywhere.

What's it called ? _____

B.   This is something we use when it rains. We open it up and hold it over our heads. It keeps us dry.

What do we call it ? _____

Introductory Exercise Two

Fill in the blanks with the words or phrases in **bold type**.

The word I'm looking for   It's called
Is it   We   Oh

1. A: _____ is the name for an animal.
2. B: _____ a wild animal?
3. A: No, not usually. _____ keep it at our house. It hates cats.
4. B: _____ ! I know what it is. _____ a dog?
5. A: That's it!

Do you mean   used for   It has   thing

6. B: It's a _____ . _____ an iron head and a wooden handle.
7. A: What's it _____ ?
8. B: It's used for hitting things.
9. A: _____ a hammer?
10. B: Right.

You mean   very fast   What do you call   It looks

11. A: _____ the thing we use to cook something quickly ?
12. B: _____ a stove ?
13. A: No. _____ like a TV. And it cooks food _____ .
14. B: Oh, of course! A microwave oven.

You mean   whachamacallit   gadget   thingamajig

15. A: Please give me the, uh, _____ .
16. B: Which thing?
17. A: The _____ we use to hold papers together.
18. B: Oh, a paper clip ?
19. A: No, not that thing. I need to put a small metal _____ into these four pieces of paper to hold them together.
20. B: I see. _____ a staple. You need a stapler.

Answers for Introductory Exercise One: A. newspaper; *B.* umbrella.

Student A

Step 1. *Describe.* Read the descriptions to Student B. (Don't tell the answer.)

1. The word I'm looking for is a person. (answer: *parent*).
2. What do you call this thing? We can listen to music or the news on it. (answer: *radio*).

Step 2. *Choose.* Listen to Student B. Ask questions to learn which of these words Student B is describing.

moon   Mexico   sun   cloud   Canada

Step 3. *Describe.* Describe these words to Student B.

1. shoe   2. hair   3. clock   4. suitcase   5. car

Step 4. *Choose.* Listen to Student B. Ask questions to learn which of these words Student B is describing.

news   basketball   singer   bird   alcohol
rain   snow   lunch   ghost   accident
hand

Step 5. *Describe and Guess.* Take turns. First describe a word to Student B; then listen to Student B and guess the word which is described.

1. sport	7. wedding	13. tourist	19. bank
3. tooth	9. China	15. diamond	21. holiday
5. clothes	11. college	17. plastic	23. park

Student B

Step 1. *Choose.* Listen to Student A. Ask questions to learn which of these words Student A is describing.

teacher   television   parent   radio   doctor

Step 2. *Describe.* Read the descriptions to Student A. (Don't tell the answer.)

1. What do you call this thing in the sky. (answer: cloud)
2. This is a country. (answer: Canada)

Step 3. *Choose.* Listen to Student A. Ask questions to learn which of these words Student A is describing.

watch   shoe   clock   car   suitcase
box   bus   hair   hat   socks
star

Step 4. *Describe.* Describe these words to Student A.

1. snow   2. accident   3. news   4. ghost   5. bird

Step 5. *Describe and Guess.* Take turns. First describe a word to Student A; then listen to Student A and guess the word which is described.

2. passport   8. money   14. pet   20. spaghetti
4. tennis   10. apartment   16. Asia   22. map
6. smoke   12. postcard   18. vegetable   24. glasses

◇ **Word Explorers** ◇

What does __ mean?
How do you spell that?
Does it have a synonym or antonym?
Is there another form of the word?
Can you give me an example?
What kind of word is it, a noun or a verb?

See the teacher's introduction on page 112.

Introductory Exercise One

Fill in the blanks with the words in bold type.

does "politician" mean   I've got it   form of the word
me an example   Do you understand

1. A: I don't think politicians are very honest.
2. B: "Politician?" What _____ ?
3. A: Someone who is chosen to be in the government.
4. B: Can you give _____ ?
5. A: Like a president or prime minister.
6. B: Hmmmm. Is there another _____ ?
7. A: Yes. _____ "politics"?
8. B: Oh, sure. _____ . "Politics" and "politician."

spell that   the opposite, too
You're what   synonym or antonym   "sick"

 9. A: My doctor said I'm healthy.

10. B: _____ ?

11. A: Healthy.

12. B: How do you _____ ?

13. A: H-E-A-L-T-H-Y.

14. B: I don't know that word. Does it have a _____ ?

15. A: An antonym is _____ . Or "ill" is _____ .

16. B: I see.

Introductory Exercise Two

noun   article   verb   adjective   adverb   preposition

The answers to these questions are on page 56.

17. A: That's frivolous.
     B: What kind of word is "frivolous"?
     A: It's an _____ .

18. A: What's wrong with this sentence?: "New York is in United States."
     B: It needs an _____ .

19. A: Do you have a doodad?
     B: What kind of word is "doodad"?
     A: It's a _____ .

20. A: Do you say, "I live at Main Street" or "on Main Street"?
     B: The correct _____ is "on."

21. A: You talk too fastly.
     B: Actually, the _____ is "fast," not "fastly."

22. A: Is there a _____ form for "explorer"?
     B: Yes, there is. It's "explore."

Student A

Step 1. Read these sentences to your partner and answer your partner's questions.

1. In Africa, there are a lot of problems with hunger.
2. My favorite animal is the tiger.
3. My aunt writes fiction.
4. My sister is always cheerful.
5. My hobby is photography.
6. Do you have any pets?
7. I like to eat junk food when I study.
8. I like spring, because it's cool.
9. Your answer is correct.

Step 2. Listen to your partner's sentences. Pretend that you don't know one of the words. Ask some questions using the "explorers."

10. Ask for the spelling of "movies." Then ask for an example.
11. Ask what kind of word "exam" is: noun, verb, etc. Then ask if it has a synonym or antonym.
12.-17. Ask some questions with "word explorers."

Step 3. With your partner, write some sentences with difficult words in the space below.

Step 4. Find a new partner and read your sentences. Also, listen to your partner's sentences and ask questions using the "explorers."

Student B

Step 1. Listen to your partner's sentences. Pretend that you don't know one of the words. Ask some questions using the "explorers."

1. Ask for the meaning of "hunger." Then ask if there is another form of the word.
2. Ask for the spelling of "tiger." Then ask what kind of word it is: noun, verb, etc.
3. Ask what "fiction" means. Then ask if it has a synonym or antonym.

4.-9. Ask some questions with "word explorers."

Step 2. Read these sentences to your partner and answer your partner's questions.

10. I like movies with a lot of action.
11. The teacher gave us an exam.
12. My friend was robbed.
13. I like to read romance novels.
14. We need to write the names alphabetically.
15. I hate it.
16. My sister quit her job.
17. My brother is a medical student.

Step 3. With your partner, write some sentences with difficult words in the space below.

Step 4. Find a new partner and read your sentences. Also, listen to your partner's sentences and ask questions using the "explorers."

Answers for Introductory Exercise Two: 17. adjective; *18.* article;
19. noun; *20.* preposition; *21.* adverb; *22.* verb.

◇ **Correctors** ◇

Are you sure?
Actually, I think you mean ___ .
Actually, ___ .
Don't you mean ___ ?
Excuse me, but ___ ?
But ___ is ___ , isn't it?

See the teacher's introduction on page 113.

Introductory Exercise One

Fill in the blanks with the words or phrases in **bold type**.

see   really true   Are you sure

right   Excuse me, but   you mean

1. A: I can't study in January. It's too hot.
2. B: _____ ? Don't _____ July?
3. A: You're _____ . I mean July is too hot.

♦ ♦ ♦ ♦ ♦ ♦ ♦ ♦

4. B: I heard that all Americans have blond hair.
5. A: _____ that's not _____ . Some have black, brown, or red hair.
6. B: I _____ .

♦ ♦ ♦ ♦ ♦ ♦ ♦ ♦

What did I say   right   actually, I was
But   is in

7. A: I love traveling in Asia. In fact, England is my favorite country there.
8. B: _____ England _____ Europe, isn't it?
9. A: Oh yeah. _____ ?
10. B: Asia.

◆   ◆   ◆   ◆   ◆   ◆   ◆   ◆

11. A: You were born in 1956, _____ ?
12. B: No, _____ born in 1965.
13. A: Oh!

Introductory Exercise Two

Correct these statements. The correct answers are on page 60.

14. A: There are 52 states in the U.S.
    B: Don't you mean _____ ?
15. A: World War II ended in 1948.
    B: Excuse me, but didn't it end in _____ ?
16. A: Berlin is in East Germany.
    B: Actually, I think you mean _____ . It is one country now.
17. A: Elephants are the largest animals on Earth.
    B: Are you sure? Aren't _____ the largest?
18. A: December 21 is the longest day of the year in London.
    B: But it's the _____ day, isn't it?

Student A

Step 1. Read these sentences to your partner and correct their sentences using the "correctors."

  1. My brother needs glasses. He can't hear very well.
  3. I really like Chinese food, especially hamburgers.
  5. Summer is my favorite month.
  7. My father bought a German car. It's a Toyota.
  9. I always eat breakfast at 7 p.m.
11. I'm planning to go to Canada to visit Disney World.
13. My sister just had a birthday. He's 15 years old.
15. My friend likes wearing dark colors, like red and yellow.

Step 2. With your partner, write some sentences with mistakes in the space below.

Step 3. Find a new partner and read your sentences. Also, listen to your partner's sentences and use the "correctors."

Student B

Step 1. Listen to your partner and correct their sentences using the "correctors." Also, read these sentences to your partner.

2. The biggest city in the U.S. is Miami.
4. My brother is a university student. She's a business major.
6. I'd like to watch a movie. Can you turn on the radio?
8. Carrots are my favorite fruit.
10. I like winter sports a lot, especially swimming.
12. I'd like to go to Africa to see some koala bears.
14. I'm hungry for something salty, like ice cream.
16. We're planning to fly from New York to Rome. The train ticket costs $1,000.

Step 2. With your partner, write some sentences with mistakes in the space below.

Step 4. Find a new partner and read your sentences. Also, listen to your partner's sentences and use the "correctors."

Answers to Introductory Exercise Two: 14. 50; *15.* 1945; *16.* Germany; *17.* whales; *18.* shortest.

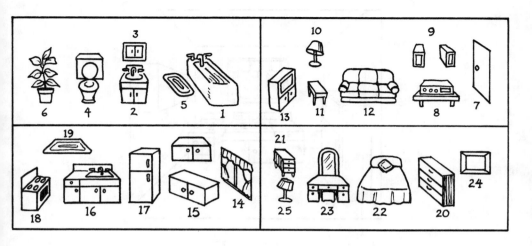

◇ **Elicitations** ◇

Do you see it?	Have you got it?
◆ **Yes, I see it.**	◆ **Got it.**
Do you understand?	**Have you found it?**
◆ **Yes, I see.**	◆ **Yeah, found it.**
	◆ **Not yet.**

Vocabulary

Bathroom
1. b_____
2. s_____
3. m _____ c_____
4. t_____
5. b_____ m _____
6. pl _____

Living Room
7. d_____
8. st_____
9. sp_____
10. l_____
11. t_____
12. s_____
13. t_____

Kitchen
14. w_____
15. c_____
16. s_____
17. r_____
18. st_____
19. r_____

Bedroom
20. ch_____
21. t_____
22. b_____
23. dr_____
24. p_____
25. l_____

See the teacher's introduction on page 113.

Correct answers are on page 62.

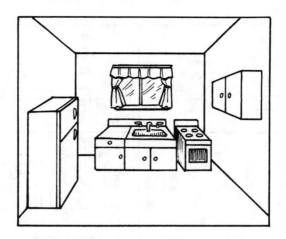

Introductory Exercise

Fill in the blanks with the words or phrases in **bold type**.

Did you say　Have you＿＿＿it?　Do you＿＿＿the place
found　Yes, that's

1. A:　On the far wall there's a window. ＿＿＿＿＿ got ＿＿＿＿＿?
2. B:　Where on the wall is it?
3. A:　In the middle, and there's a curtain hanging on it. ＿＿＿＿＿
　　　see ＿＿＿＿?
4. B:　＿＿＿＿＿＿＿＿＿ a curtain?
5. A:　＿＿＿＿＿＿＿＿＿＿ right. And there's a sink under it.
　　　Also, against the far wall there's a stove. It's in the corner on the
　　　right. Have you ＿＿＿＿＿ it?

I've got it　understand　On which　not yet

6. B:　No, ＿＿＿＿＿. Is the stove almost touching the sink?
7. A:　Yes, but there's a space between them. Also, there's a cabinet on
　　　the right wall.
8. B:　＿＿＿＿＿ wall?
9. A:　On the right wall. The refrigerator is against the left wall. Do
　　　you ＿＿＿＿＿?
10. B:　Yes, ＿＿＿＿＿＿＿＿＿＿＿.

Answers: 1. bathtub, *2.* sink (or basin), *3.* medicine cabinet, *4.* toilet, *5.* bathmat,
6. plant, *7.* door, *8.* stereo, *9.* speakers, *10.*(table) lamp, *11.* (side) table, *12.* sofa,
13. television (TV), *14.* window, *15.* cabinets, *16.* (kitchen) sink, *17.* refrigerator,
18. stove, *19.* rug, *20.* chest (of drawers, or bureau), *21.* (bedside) table (or night stand),
22. bed, *23.* dresser (or dressing table), *24.* picture, *25.* (bedside) lamp.

Student A

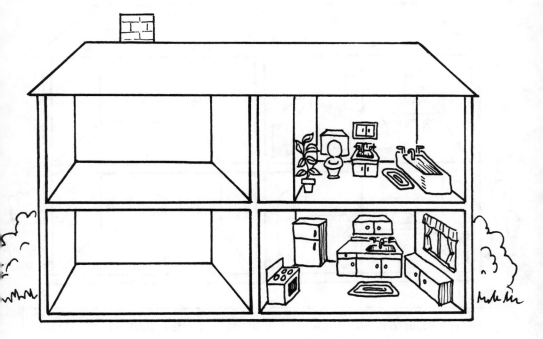

Step 1. *Bathroom.* Read the bathroom description to Student B. Elicit confirmations. Student B will draw it.

Draw the bathroom. Against the far wall, in the middle, there's a sink. Over the sink, there's a medicine cabinet. On the left side of the sink, in the corner, is the toilet. On the right side of the sink, in the corner, is the bathtub. On the floor beside the bathtub, there's a bathmat. Against the left wall, there's a plant on the floor.

Step 2. *Living Room.* Student B will describe the living room. Listen, respond, and draw it.

Step 3. *Kitchen.* Describe the kitchen to Student B. Elicit confirmations. Student B will draw it.

Step 4. *Bedroom.* Listen to Student B, respond, and draw the bedroom.

Student B

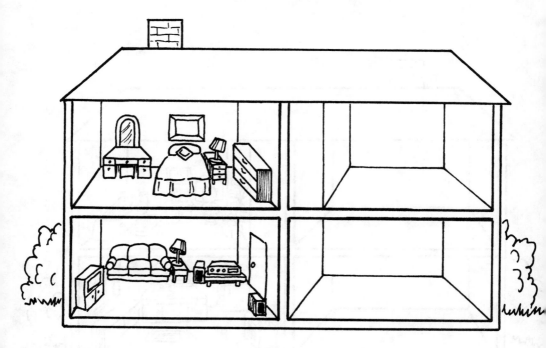

Step 1. *Bathroom*. Student A will describe the bathroom. Listen, respond, and draw it.

Step 2. *Living Room*. Read the living room description to Student A. Elicit confirmations. Student A will draw it.

Against the far wall, on the left, in the corner, is a sofa. Next to the sofa and touching it is a small table. On it, there's a lamp. Also against the far wall, but on the right, in the corner, is a small table with a stereo on it. On the left side of the stereo, on the floor, is a stereo speaker. On the right wall, there's a door in the middle of the wall. On the right side of the door, against the wall, is another speaker. The TV is in the middle of the left wall.

Step 3. *Kitchen*. Listen to Student A, respond, and draw the kitchen.

Step 4. *Bedroom*. Describe the bedroom to Student A. Elicit confirmations. Student A will draw it.

◇ Starting and Stopping ◇ a Conversation

Conversation Starters

Excuse me, I like your ___.
Are you a friend of ___?
Could I ask you something?
Could/can I ask ___?

See the teacher's introduction on page 114.

Introductory Exercise

Fill in the blanks with the words or phrases in **bold type**.

something   Could   teacher   Do you think

In a classroom before class starts:

1. A: Excuse me. _____ I ask you _____? Do
   you know the _____ for this class?

2. B: Yeah.

3. A: _____ she's a good teacher?

4. B: Yes, I do. My friends all say that she's helpful.

How about you   him a long time   a friend of Jim's
I like your   Can I ask

At a party at Jim's apartment:

5. A: Hi. Are you _____ ?

6. B: Yeah, I am. Jim and I work together. _____?

7. A: I just moved into the next apartment. Have you known _____?

8. B: About 5 years.

In a waiting room:

9 A: Hi. _____ shirt.

10. B: Thanks.

11. A: _____ where you got it?

12. B: Sure. I got it at the mall downtown.

Conversation Stoppers

Would you excuse me?
Well, I'd better be going/ I should be going.
(It's been) nice talking to you
I hope we get a chance to talk again sometime.

Fill in the blanks with the words or phrases in **bold type**.

see you   nice talking   you excuse   get a chance
It's been   I'd better

In a classroom:

1. A: I think the teacher is ready to start. It's been _____ to you.

2. B: Yeah. I enjoyed it too.

3. A: I haven't had a chance to talk to Tom yet. Would _____ me?

4. B: Sure.

5. A: _____ nice talking to you; _____ later.

In a waiting room:

6. B: Well, I won't take up any more of your time.

    _____ be going.

7. A: I hope we _____ to talk again sometime..

8. B: Me too.

Student A

Step 1. Read the situations to Student B, who will begin a conversation with you. Then have a 1½ minute conversation with B. After 1½ minutes, **end the conversation.** (Then the teacher will tell you to talk to a different Student B.)

1. Tell Student B, "We're sitting next to each other on an airplane. I'm a businessperson."

2. Tell Student B, "We're in a classroom. I'm a female student."

3. Tell Student B, "We're at a party at your uncle's house. I'm an older man. We're standing near each other."

4. Tell Student B, "We're at a park. I'm a child sitting next to you on a park bench."

5. Tell Student B, "We're at a meeting for new foreign students. Before the meeting starts, you see me standing alone. I look lonely."

6. Tell Student B, "We're in the waiting room of a doctor's office. I'm just sitting here. I look worried."

Step 2. Listen to B. Then **start a conversation** with B and talk for 1½ minutes. After 1½ minutes, **end the conversation**.

7. You are a professional athlete.

8. You are a new student from California.

9. You are a famous musician.

10. You are a foreign student at the beginning level of English.

11. You are a housewife with eight children.

Student B

Step 1. Listen to Student A. **Start a conversation** with A and talk for 1½ minutes. After 1½ minutes, **end the conversation**. (Then, the teacher will tell you to talk to a different Student A.)

1. You are traveling to Europe for a vacation.
2. You are a male student. You are worried about passing this class.
3. You are a female, about 16 years old.
4. You are a man, about 25 years old.
5. You are a foreign student. You have been at this college three years.
6. You are a pregnant woman.

Step 2. Read the situations to Student A. Then have a 1½-minute conversation with A. After 1½ minutes, **end the conversation**.

7. Tell Student A, "We're at a party at your best friend's house. I'm a beautiful woman. We're standing near each other."

8. Tell Student A, "We're the only two people in a classroom on the first day of school. We have to wait for about 15 minutes for class to begin. You think that perhaps I'm the teacher."

9. Tell Student A, "We're at a concert. We have to wait for about 10 minutes for the concert to begin. We're the same age."

10. Tell Student A, "We live in the same apartment building. We're waiting for a bus in front of the building. I'm an English teacher."

11. Tell Student A, "We're in the waiting room of a dentist's office. I'm just sitting here. I look bored."

◇ Beginning and Ending ◇ a Phone Call

Beginnings

Formal: *to a teacher, boss, etc.*

Phone: Ring, Ring
Teacher: Hello.
Student: Hello. **Could I speak** to Mr. Smith, please?
Teacher: This is Mr. Smith.
Student: Hello, Mr. Smith. This is Ann Mugabe.
    Am **I bothering you by calling** now?
Teacher: No, I'm free to talk now.

Informal/friendly: *to a friend*

Phone: Ring, Ring
Parent: Hello.
Student: Hello. **Could I speak** to Tom?
Parent: Sure. Just a moment.
Tom: Hello.
Student: **Hi**, Tom. **This is** Toru. **I'm calling to see if**
    you can ___ .

Direct: *to a store, theater, etc.*

Phone: Ring, Ring
Salesperson: Ace Records.
Student: **Hi. Could you tell me** if you sell CDs?

See the teacher's introduction on page 114.

Endings

Formal: *to a teacher, boss, etc.*
   Student: **I don't want to take up any more of your time. Thank you for your help.**
   Teacher: You're welcome.
   Student: Goodbye.

Informal/friendly: *to a friend*
   Student: Well, **I'd better let you go.**
   Friend: OK. I'll talk to you later.
   Student: OK. Bye.

Direct: *to a store, theater, etc.*
   Student: **Thanks for the information.**
   Salesperson: You're welcome.
   Student: Bye.

Other Useful Telephone Expressions

I heard about you from a friend of mine.
I read in the newspaper that you were having a sale.
Could you tell me how much the charge is?

Introductory Exercise

Fill in the blanks with the words or phrases in **bold type**.

       make up   **do for you**   **This is**   **I'll see you**
       one of   **bad time**   **hope I'm not**   **Thank you**

A student is calling a teacher.

1. *Phone:* Ring, Ring
2. *Teacher:* Hello.
3. *Student:* Hello, Mr. Jones? _____ Fred Smith.
   I'm _____ your history students.
4. *Teacher:* Yes, Fred. What can I _____ ?
5. *Student:* I _____ calling at a _____ .
6. *Teacher:* No, I'm not busy now.

7. *Student:* I was absent yesterday morning, and I'm calling to see if I could _____ the test I missed.
8. *Teacher:* Sure. Can you take it tomorrow at noon?
9. *Student:* That will be fine. _____ very much.
   _____ tomorrow.
10. *Teacher:* OK, see you tomorrow.
11. *Student:* Goodbye.
12. *Teacher:* Goodbye.

how much you charge   call you back later   see
just to get   heard about you from a friend

A student is calling a car shop.

13. *Worker:* Ben's Auto Shop.
14. *Student:* I _____ of mine. He says that you do good auto work. Do you change oil?
15. *Worker:* Yes, we do.
16. *Student:* Could you tell me _____ ?
17. *Worker:* $18.
18. *Student:* I _____ . Right now I'm calling _____ the price. I'll _____ to make an appointment.
19. *Worker:* Thanks for calling.
20. *Student:* Sure. Bye.

Could I speak   calling   moment
bothering   let you go

A student is calling a dormitory.

21. *Voice:* Hello. Bolton Dorm.
22. *Ali:* _____ to Maria Gonzalez, please?
23. *Voice:* Just a _____ , please.
24. *Maria:* Hello?
25. *Ali:* Hi, Maria. This is Ali. I'm _____ about the assignment. I hope I'm not _____ you.
26. *Maria:* No, not at all. I'm doing it now. It's Lesson 32.
27. *Ali:* Ok. Thanks a lot. I'd better _____ .
28. *Maria:* Bye.

Student A

Step 1. You are making a phone call. You start by saying "Ring, ring."

1. You are calling the theater to find out what movie is playing, what time it starts, and how much tickets cost.

2. You were absent from your English class today. You are calling your classmate, Ken, to find out what happened in class.

3. You are feeling sick. You call Dr. Green to make an appointment. Your friend, Mark Jones, said he was a very good doctor.

4. You want to make reservations for dinner at a restaurant, *The French Chef*, for you and three friends.

5. You want to buy a pair of Nike running shoes. Call the sport shop, *Sports for All*, to find out the prices.

6. You are calling your classmate, Ann, to invite her to go to a movie with you.

Step 2. Answer the phone and talk to Student B.

7. You are Terry's mother. Terry is not at home.

8. You work at *The Hair Place*. You are a hairdresser.

9. You are Mrs. Smith, a science teacher.

10. You are Bill. You just returned from a trip to a foreign country.

11. You are a police officer.

Step 3. With your partner, take turns calling each other for information. Use the "Yellow Pages" and find out what these businesses do.

▶ **Abrasives**

DOWD SUPPLY CO.
Grassy Brook Rd. Newfane 802 365-4346

▶ **Amusement Devices**

LYLA CORP. 143 North Ave. Burlington
Toll Free — Dial "1" & Then 800 343-4113

▶ **Animal Control**

Paul's Pest Control
COMPLETE CONTROL SERVICES &
INSPECTIONS. SERVING AREA SINCE 1979
Bellows Falls, VT 802 463-4064

▶ **Armored Car Service**

BERKSHIRE ARMORED CAR SERVICE, INC.
Collecting and Banking Deposits
Courier Service
Mail Delivery ● Coin Wrapping
Anywhere in New England
All Risk Insurance Provided
ATM Service
Full Service Money Processing
"FOR INFORMATION CALL"
56½ Merchants Row Rutland **802 773-3211**

▶ **Balloons — Novelty & Toy**

BALLOONS OVER BRATTLEBORO
BALLOONS FOR ALL OCCASIONS
● WE SHIP TO ALL 50 STATES
● BALLOON DECORATING
● BALLOON-IN-A-BOX
● MASTERCARD ● VISA ● AMEX
60 Elliott Brattleboro 802 254-8493

▶ **Beads**

Bead Outlet The 216 Canal Bratt 802 257-2461

▶ **Bonsai**

See Plants — Retail

▶ **Cartoonists**

ANDREW TOOS *Hilarious Illustrations*
8 Laurel Sherman Ct. Tel & Fax 203 350-3718

▶ **Chimney Sweeps**

CHIMNEY DOCTOR THE
Ian Conway — Master Sweep
● Year-round Service
● Cleaning - Repair - Relining
● Stove & Prefab Chimney Installations
● Member National Sweeps Guild
Westminster VT 802 387-6037

▶ **Games & Game Supplies**

ADVANCE WHIP & NOVELTY CO INC
Merchandise & Games on Consignment
Complete Line of Bingo & Poker Supplies
330 Elm Westfield MA 413 562-9666

▶ **Kites**

BLUE SKY'S KITE CONNECTION
Northgate Plz Peterborough NH **603 924-9448**

▶ **Land Clearing and Leveling**

INMAN CLIFF Hubbard Hill Rd W Hall 368-2335

▶ **Lasers**

Nippon-American Inc Putney VT 802 287-5210

▶ **Night Clubs**

TWIN PEAKS Rte 100 Wil 802 464-7422

▶ **Organs — Renting**

COMMUNITY MUSIC OF NEW ENGLAND
● Low cost instrument leases & repairs
● We buy, sell & trade new and used woodwinds,
brass, and strings
Putney Toll Free 800 962-0090

▶ **Plants Retail**

Designing Women Rt 100 W. Dover 802 464-6552
Windham Flowers 143 Main Bratt 802 257-1411

▶ **Plaques**

ENGRAVE IT
10 West St Keene NH 603 352-8559

▶ **Quilts**

Anton of Vt Quilts & Fabrics Ward 802 896-6007
Carriage House Comforters Rte 30 Bratt .. 802 257-0407

▶ **Rags**

See Wiping Cloths

▶ **Religious Goods**

Whispering Hope Christian Book Store
Putney Rd Bratt 802 254-3889

▶ **Rest Homes**

Bert Anne Convalescent Home
West Chesterfield NH 256-6277
Hilltop House Bradley Ter Bratt 254-5524
Lovely Hill Reservoir Rd Pawling NY 914 255-6666

▶ **Rubber Stamps**

RUBBER STAMPS OF AMERICA
Academy Av Saxtons River 802 869-2622

▶ **Schools**

MISS SUZI'S SCHOOL OF BEAUTY AND CHARM
3000½ Mt Snow Drive Dover Vt 800 366-4775
WORLD LEARNING INC AND SCHOOL FOR
INTL TRAINING Kipling Rd Bratt 802 257-7751

▶ **Steeple Jacks**

SKYLINE ENGINEERS INC
Specialists in Restoration & Repairs
STEEPLES ● TOWERS ● DOMES
GOLD LEAFING ● MAXONRY
24 HR. EMERGENCY SERVICE
58 East St Fitchburg MA **508-342-7000**

▶ **Tablets & Plaques**

See Plaques

▶ **Theatrical Hats**

BROADWAY COSTUME CO
20,000 Costumes—Individual UPS Delivery
186 South St Boston Ma 617 426-3560
Costume Ladies Canal St Bratt 257-2628

▶ **Toupees**

FULLER HAIR FOR GUYS AND GALS
7 Ashuelot Keene NH 603 352-9002

▶ **Windsurfing**

NEW ENGLAND SAILBOARD CO
Main Jamaica 802 874-4178
Timing House Ski Shop The Wil 802 464-3376

▶ **Wiping Cloths**

ERC Wiping Products
Diapers - Towels - Rags - Overnight Service
875 Washington Canton Ma
Toll Free — Dial "1" then 800 225-9473

▶ **Zipper — Repairing**

Fabricare Brookside Plz Bratt 802 254-5400

Student B

Step 1. Answer the phone and talk to Student A.

1. You work at a movie theater called Cinemax.
2. You are Ken. You are a student.
3. You are a receptionist. You work in Dr. Green's office.
4. You are a worker at *The French Chef*, a restaurant.
5. You work at a sports shop called *Sports for All*.
6. You are Ann, a student.

Step 2. You are making a phone call. You start by saying "Ring, ring."

7. You want to invite your friend, Terry, to your house for dinner.
8. You are calling *The Hair Place* to find out how much they charge for a cut. You don't want to make an appointment yet. You heard about *The Hair Place* from your friend, Ken.
9. Your science teacher, Mrs. Smith, told you to buy a book, but you forgot the title. You are calling her.
10. You are calling your friend, Bill, to find out how his trip was.
11. You are calling the police station because you lost your passport.

Step 3. With your partner, take turns calling each other for information. Use the "Yellow Pages" and find out what these businesses do.

◇ <u>Expressing Opinions</u> ◇

Statements

In my opinion —	**Don't you think** —
It seems to me —	**According to** —
I feel —	

Agreements

I agree.	**That's right/true.**
You're right.	**That's a good point.**

Disagreements

I'm afraid I disagree.	**Maybe/Perhaps, but** —
I'm not sure I agree.	**I don't agree.**

See the teacher's introduction on page 115.

Introductory Exercise

Fill in the blanks with the words or phrases in **bold type**.

Perhaps   true   afraid I disagree   my opinion

1. A: In _____ , camping is more fun than swimming.

2. B: I'm _____ . I think camping is a little dangerous.

3. A: _____ , but if you're careful, you'll have no problems.

4. B: That's _____ .

it seems   not sure I agree   That's a good
I feel   You're right

5. A: _____ pets are good for children.

6. B: _____ point. Having pets teaches kids to be
responsible. But _____ to me pets are a lot of work.

7. A: I'm _____ . Some pets, like fish, are easy.

8. B: _____ . But most kids want dogs or cats.

I don't agree   I agree   According to   Don't you think

9. A: _____ we should stop doing business with the country
of Xanadu?

10. B: _____ completely. Xanadu doesn't respect human rights.

11. C: I'm sorry, but _____ with either of you.
We need to maintain contact if we want to influence them.

12. A: _____ a recent poll, most people
agree with our point of view.

Agree or disagree with these statements.

13.   In my opinion, people should not own guns.

_____

14.   Don't you think everyone should go to school until the age of eighteen?

_____

15.   American football is stupid.

_____

16.   I feel there's too much violence on TV.

_____

Student A

Step 1. First fill in the blanks. Then say your sentences to Student B. After Student B answers, give reasons for your opinions.

1. I feel _____ is the best city in the world.
2. In my opinion, _____ is the best season.
3. Don't you think girls are harder workers than boys?
4. It seems to me you're the best student in this class.
5. I feel _____ is the most exciting sport to watch.
6. According to many travel agents, group tours are the best way to travel.

Step 2. Listen to Student B, choose one response, and give reasons for your opinion.

Agree	*Disagree*
7. You're right.	Perhaps, but . . .
8. That's a good point.	I'm not sure I agree.
9. I agree.	I'm afraid I disagree.
10. That's right.	I don't agree.
11. True.	Maybe, but . . .

Step 3. With your partner, write several sentences in the space below, giving your opinion. Use the opinion statements.

Step 4. Find new partners and read your opinions to them. They will agree or disagree with you. Give the reasons for your opinion.

Student B

Step 1. Listen to Student A, choose one response, and give reasons for your opinion.

Agree	*Disagree*
1. I agree.	I'm afraid I disagree.
2. That's true.	I'm not sure I agree.
3. That's a good point.	Perhaps, but . . .
4. That's right.	I don't agree.
5. You're right.	I'm not sure I agree.
6. I agree.	I'm afraid I disagree.

Step 2. First fill in the blanks. Then say your sentences to Student A. After Student A answers, give reasons for your opinion.

7. Don't you think single life is better than married life?
8. In my opinion, _____ is the best country in the world.
9. I feel TV is _____ .
10. It seems to me you work too hard.
11. According to many psychologists, 30 years old is a good age to get married.

Step 3. With your partner, write several sentences in the space below giving your opinion. Use the opinion statements.

Step 4. Find new partners and read your opinions to them. They will agree or disagree with you. Give the reasons for your opinion.

◇ **Making a** ◇ **Group Decision**

Proposals
Why don't we ___
We could ___
Let's ___

Considerations
Sounds good.
I'd rather not.
I don't care.
It doesn't matter to me.

See the teacher's introduction on page 115.

Introductory Exercise

Fill in the blanks with the words or phrases in **bold type**.

sounds good   We could   I don't care
I'd rather   What do you want to do

1. A: _____ this weekend? Should we go to
   the Boston Pops or "Nunsense"?

2. B: _____ . How about you?

3. A: I enjoy comedies, so "Nunsense" _____ to me.

4. B: Actually, _____ go to the Boston Pops. They're having a tribute to Duke Ellington, which could be great.

5. A: That's true, but I'd really like to see a comedy.

6. B: _____ do both, if they aren't too expensive.

doesn't matter to me   Let's
Why don't   Sounds

7. A: _____ we call to find out the prices?

8. B: Good idea. Should we invite someone to go with us?

9. A: It _____ .

10. B: _____ call some friends. What do you think?

11. A: _____ good.

Group Work

Step 1. Get in groups of 3 or 4 students. Student A is the first "score keeper" for 8 minutes. The score keeper will:

a. choose one of the topics from pages 82-84 for the others to discuss;

b. tell the members when 8 minutes is finished;

c. mark each time a group member uses one of the expressions on the score sheet.

The score keeper will *not* join the discussion.

SCORE SHEET				
Expressions	*Student A*	*Student B*	*Student C*	*Student D*
Why don't we ___ ?				
We could ___ .				
Let's ___ .				
Sounds good.				
I'd rather (not) ___ .				
I don't care.				
It doesn't matter to me.				

Step 2. Student B is the score keeper for 8 minutes.

Step 3. Student C is the score keeper for 8 minutes.

Step 4. Get in new groups with different partners and compare the decisions you made during your discussions.

Topics for Discussion

Topic 1: Plan a vacation together using these:

Topic 2: Choose one of these to attend together:

Topic 3. You want to spend a weekend with your classmates. Decide which one of these would be best to stay in.

LODGING ▣ LODGING ▣ LODGING

ACCOMMODATIONS
ACCOMMODATIONS
ACCOMMODATIONS

▣

ACCOMMODATIONS

	Number of Guest Rooms	Price Range/Double	Waterbeds	Children Free Under Age	Non-Smoking Rooms	On-Site Restaurant	Cable/Satellite TV	Indoor Pool	Fitness Center/Sauna	Fireplace	Pets Allowed	Handicap Accessible	Kitchen/Kitchenettes	Meeting Rooms	Courtesy Van	Packages
Antlers Motel	33	$44-46		12	•	•	•					•			•	
Best Western Midway Hotel	110	$64-79		18	•	•	•	•	•			•		•	•	•
Comfort Inn	56	$40-48		18	•		•	•	•		•	•	•			
Days Inn	136	$46-59		17	•	•	•	•	•		•	•		•	•	•
Daystop	46	$34-43		13	•		•					•	•			
Eau Claire Motel	24	$26-36		18	•	•	•			•		•				
Evenox Motel	26	$36		18	•		•					•				
Exel Inn of Eau Claire	102	$35-37	•	18			•				•	•		•		
Green Tree Inn	24	$40-60		12	•		•			•		•	•	•		
Hampton Inn (opening May '92)	106	$38-54		12	•		•	•				•				•
Heartland Inn	90	$45	•	16	•		•		•		•	•		•		•
Heritage Motel	28	$34-38	•	14			•				•	•				
Holiday Inn Gateway	244	$53-72		18	•	•	•	•			•	•		•	•	•
Howard Johnson Lodge	120	$54-65	•	18	•	•	•	•	•		•	•		•		•
Maple Manor Motel	34	$30-40	•	18	•	•					•	•	•			•
Westgate Motel	27	$30-35		12	•		•					•	•			
Woodland Motel	9	$28		6	•						•			•		•
Bed & Breakfast Inns																
Apple Tree Inn	4	$75-125								•			•		•	•
Fanny Hill Victorian Inn	7	$69-139			•	•	•			•			•	•	•	•

◇ **Connectors** ◇

How come?	**I see.**
How about you?	**You mean __?**
What does __ mean?	**You think __?**
Can you explain __?	**Good point.**

See the teacher's introduction on page 116.

Introductory Exercise

Fill in the blanks with the words in **bold type**.

How come   Really   How about you   I see   you mean

1. ***Leader:*** Are you ready to start? The topic I'd like to discuss is movies. Here's my first question: How often do you watch movies? Either of you can answer first.

2. ***Group member B:*** Do _____ at the movie theater or on TV?

3. ***Leader:*** Either one.

4. ***Group member B:*** Then I'd say I watch five movies a week.

5. ***Group member A:*** _____? Do you have that much free time?

6. ***Group member B:*** Sure. I always record movies and then watch part of one before I go to bed. _____?

7. ***Group member A:*** I probably watch about one movie a month.

8. ***Leader:*** _____? Why not more?

9. *Group member A:* I prefer to see movies at a theater rather than on TV, and I can afford to go only once a month. How about you, Mr./Ms. Leader?

10. *Leader:* I'm in the middle of both of you. I watch one movie a week.

11. *Group member A:* _____ .

I'd have to think about that for a while
Can you explain   you think   Excuse me
What does ____ mean   I see   Here's my next question
How about you   good points

12. *Leader:* _____: Would you like to be an actor?

13. *Group member A:* No. I once tried to be in a play and had to quit because I was too scared. _____ , B?

14. *Group member B:* _____ .
 What do _____, Mr./Ms. Leader?

15. *Leader:* I think it would be great! You could travel a lot, make a lot of money, and meet famous people.

16. *Group member B:* Those are _____, but don't you think the work would be hard?

17. *Leader:* Not really. I've never had stage fright.

18. *Group member A:* _____ . _____
 "stage fright" _____?

19. *Leader:* Do you know how to explain it, B?

20. *Group member B:* Yes, it means to be afraid to talk or act in front of a lot of people.

21. *Group member A:* _____. Thanks. So, Mr./Ms. Leader, have you ever been in a play?

22. *Leader:* Yes and no.

23. *Group member B:* _____ what you mean by that?

24. *Leader:* I was "Offstage Voice" in the play *I Hear Voices.*

Student A

Step 1. You are the leader. Ask Students B and C these questions and lead a discussion. Use discussion "connectors."

Family

1. How many members are there in your family?
2. What are the advantages and disadvantages to being in your position in the family? (For example, what is the advantage/disadvantage of being the oldest or youngest child?)
3. Is there someone that you usually talk to when you have a problem?
4. When you are away from home, is there someone you especially miss?
5. As a child, how much time did you spend with your family members each week?
6. Did you have your own room as a child or did you share it?
7. Did you often take vacations with your family?
8. Was there a holiday that you especially enjoyed with your family?
9. Did both of your parents discipline you as a child when you were bad?
10. Do you have any relatives (including uncles and aunts) who are famous or very successful?
11. Which do you think are easier to raise, sons or daughters?
12. What do you think a family has to do to be happy together?

Step 2. You are a group member. Student B will be the group leader. Answer the questions, and use discussion "connectors." Try to be an active group member.

Step 3. You are a group member. Student C will be the group leader. Answer the questions, and use discussion "connectors." Try to be an active group member.

Step 4. See page 90.

Student B

Step 1. You are a group member. Student A will be the group leader. Answer the questions, and use discussion "connectors." Try to be an active group member.

Step 2. You are the leader. Ask Students A and C these questions and lead a discussion. Use discussion "connectors."

Music

1. What type of music do you enjoy the most?
2. What are the names of some of your favorite groups?
3. When was the last time you went to a concert?
4. Can you play any musical instruments?
5. What musical instrument would you like to be able to play very well?
6. Is anyone in your family very good at music?
7. Do you enjoy the same type of music as your parents?
8. Do you enjoy some traditional songs from your country?
9. When do you most enjoy listening to music (for example, during dinner or while studying)?
10. Would you feel very unhappy if you couldn't listen to music?
11. Do you think it would be interesting to have a job with music (for example, as a rock musician or radio disk jockey)?
12. Have you ever sung or played music in front of an audience?

Step 3. You are a group member. Student C will be the group leader. Answer the questions, and use discussion "connectors." Try to be an active group member.

Step 4. See page 90.

Student C

Step 1. You are a group member. Student A will be the group leader. Answer the questions, and use discussion "connectors." Try to be an active group member.

Step 2. You are a group member. Student B will be the group leader. Answer the questions, and use discussion "connectors." Try to be an active group member.

Step 3. You are the leader. Ask Students A and B these questions and lead a discussion. Use discussion "connectors."

Sports & Exercise

1. Do you get exercise every day?
2. In general, do you prefer team sports (for example, basketball) or individual sports (for example, swimming)?
3. In general, do you like to play or watch sports?
4. Which sport is your favorite to watch?
5. Do you sometimes go to a stadium to watch professional sports?
6. Do you have a friend or family member who is very good at a sport?
7. Have you ever met a professional athlete?
8. Is there a professional athlete you admire very much?
9. If possible, what sport would you like to be able to play very well?
10. When you exercise, what is your main purpose (for example, to lose weight or to get big muscles)?
11. In general, do you think the people in your country exercise enough?
12. What sports are popular in your country?

Step 4. See page 90.

Step 5. With your partners, choose a discussion topic and write several discussion questions. (Your partners' questions and your questions should be the same.) Write your questions at the bottom of the page. Then find new partners and take turns being leaders and members of a discussion group.

Possible Discussion Topics

culture shock
free time
money
food
education
shopping
this school
alcohol
this town
future job
a problem
roommates

my hometown
best friends
women working
a recent news story
best place to live
life in the dormitory
life in a foreign country
seasons & holidays
marriage & divorce
how to study a foreign language
single life/married life

Your Questions

━━━━ ◇ **Summarizers** ◇ ━━━━

In other words, ___ .   In summary ___ .
You mean ___ .   To sum up ___ .
It sounds like ___ .   In conclusion ___ .
What you're saying is (that) ___ .

See the teacher's introduction on page 117.

Introductory Exercise

Fill in the blanks with the sentences in **bold type**.

**What you're saying is that
you couldn't get us a flight.**

In other words, you were really busy.

It sounds like you enjoy traveling.

1. A: Yesterday, I couldn't do my homework. After school, I had to buy a present for my friend. On my way home, I went to the library. When I got home, I cleaned the house and got dinner. After dinner, I talked to my friends until midnight.

2. B: _____ .

3. A: Exactly.

◆　◆　◆　◆　◆　◆

4. A: I tried to make a plane reservation. There were no seats available for Sunday. On Monday, the first flight isn't until noon, which is too late. And on Tuesday, there are no flights.

5. B: _____ .

6. A: That's right.

◆   ◆   ◆   ◆   ◆   ◆

7. A: In June, I visited France for two weeks. Then I went to Italy for a week. In August, I flew to Japan and Korea. Next month, I'm planning to visit South America.

8. B: _____ .

9. A: Yes, I do.

You mean   in summary   conclusion
sums it up

10. A: So, _____ , I feel that anyone who studies English can become fluent, if one works hard enough.

11. B: _____ natural ability isn't important?

12. A: That's right. I think that that _____ .

13. B: I'm afraid I can't agree with your _____ .

Student A

Step 1. Read these to Student B. Student B will summarize.

1. This morning my alarm didn't work, so I got up late. I drove to work fast, so a policeman stopped me. Then I got to work late, and my boss was angry.
2. I've got a headache, my stomach hurts, and I feel very cold.
3. My sister called me at 7 o'clock. After we talked, my friend called me and we talked for an hour. Then my mother called me.
4. I threw my book at my brother and yelled at him. Then I left the room and shut the door hard.

Step 2. Listen to Student B. Then choose the best summary.

5. It sounds like $\begin{cases} \text{you really enjoy school.} \\ \text{you'd like me to help you.} \end{cases}$

6. You mean $\begin{cases} \text{you have a lot of energy.} \\ \text{you need a doctor.} \end{cases}$

7. In other words, $\begin{cases} \text{you're lonely.} \\ \text{you're happy.} \end{cases}$

Step 3. Take turns with your partner. One partner **secretly** chooses a topic and describes it. The other partner listens and then summarizes, using a "summarizer."

Topics to Choose From

Both partners have the same topics.

Tell about . . .

a problem in your country.

a time you were very afraid.

your favorite movie star.

a famous person in your country.

a time you were late for an appointment.

something good about your country.

a time you did something well in school.

a time you were tired.

a time you were embarrassed.

your favorite singer.

a time you were naughty.

a time you did something well in sports.

Student B

Step 1. Listen to Student A. Then choose the best summary.

1. You mean $\begin{cases} \text{you had a nice morning.} \\ \text{you had a lot of problems this morning.} \end{cases}$

2. What you are saying is that $\begin{cases} \text{you want to go home.} \\ \text{you want to play tennis.} \end{cases}$

3. In other words, $\begin{cases} \text{you talked a lot on the phone.} \\ \text{you're very busy today.} \end{cases}$

4. It sounds like $\begin{cases} \text{you were very happy.} \\ \text{you were very angry.} \end{cases}$

Step 2. Read these to Student A. Student A will summarize.

5. I'm really confused about my homework. I'm not sure how to write the introduction. Also, I think I have some grammar problems.

6. I just finished playing tennis. Now I'm going to go swimming. After that, I plan to go for a walk.

7. Usually I'm alone. I wish I had a roommate. I don't have anyone to talk to. I'd like to have someone who could listen to my problems and who could tell me theirs.

Step 3. Take turns with your partner. One partner **secretly** chooses a topic and describes it. The other partner listens and then summarizes, using a "summarizer."

Topics to Choose From

Both partners have the same topics.

Tell about . . .

a problem in your country.

a time you were very afraid.

your favorite movie star.

a famous person in your country.

a time you were late for an appointment.

something good about your country.

a time you did something well in school.

a time you were tired.

a time you were embarrassed.

your favorite singer.

a time you were naughty.

a time you did something well in sports.

◇ Conducting a Formal ◇ Meeting

Procedural Expressions

I'd like to call this meeting to order.
= *Let's start the meeting.*

Who will take the minutes?
= *Who will take notes on the meeting?*

The first topic on the agenda is . . .
= *The first thing on the list of things to do is . . .*

I move ___ .
= *I suggest ___ , and I want everyone to vote on my suggestion.*

I second the motion.
= *I support the suggestion.*

The motion is open for discussion.
= *We can begin the discussion.*

Does everyone agree that we should vote?

All in favor say "aye." (*or informal* **raise your hands**).
= *Everyone who agrees say "yes."*

All opposed say "nay" (*or informal* **raise your hands**).
= *Everyone who disagrees say "no."*

The motion has passed.
= *We will do what was suggested.*

The motion is defeated.
= *We will not do what was suggested.*

I move we adjourn.
= *I suggest that we end the meeting.*

See the teacher's introduction on page 117.

Introductory Exercise

Fill in the blanks with the words or phrases in **bold type**.

minutes   agenda   meeting to order   topic

Beginning a meeting

1.   *Chair:* I'd like to call the _____ . Roberto,

will you take the _____ ? Our first _____

on the _____ is to decide what to do for our

teacher's birthday. Does anyone have any suggestions?

is open for discussion   move   afraid I disagree

Making a motion

2.   *Member A:* I _____ that we buy a present.
Member C: I second the motion.

3.   *Chair:* OK, the motion _____ .

4.   *Member A:* The reason buying a present is a good idea is that . . .

5.   *Member B:* I'm _____ because . . .

everyone agree that we   is passed   your hands
move we vote   opposed   in favor

Voting on a suggestion

6.   *Member C:* I _____ on the motion to buy a present.

7.   *Chair:* Does _____ should vote?

8.   *Members A, B, C, & Chair:* Yes.

9.   *Chair:* All _____ of buying a present, please raise _____ .

All _____ , please raise your hands. (Chair votes too.) There

are three in favor and one opposed. The motion _____ .

**we vote on   Does everyone agree   move
motion is defeated   is open for**

Defeating a suggestion

10.   *Chair:* Now we should decide what present to buy.

11.   *Member C:* I _____ that we buy a TV.

12.   *Chair:* The motion to buy a TV _____ discussion.

13.   *Member B:* I think . . .

14.   *Member C:* In my opinion, . . .

15.   *Member A:* I move _____ buying a TV now.

16.   *Chair:* _____ we should vote?

17.   *Members A, B, C, & Chair:* Yes.

18.   *Chair:* All in favor, please say "aye." All opposed, say "nay." It's one in favor and three opposed. The _____ .
Are there any other suggestions?

is adjourned   adjourn

Adjourning a meeting

19.   *Member C:* I move we _____ the meeting.

20.   *Chair:* Does everyone agree we should adjourn?

21.   *Members A, B, C, & Chair:* Yes.

22.   *Chair:* The meeting _____ .

Step 1. Get into groups of 4–5 students. The student with the longest name will be the temporary chairperson for each group.

Step 2. Hold a business meeting to elect a chairperson.

Step 3. Each group chooses one of these topics, following formal procedures.

Topic A: Design a language program.
    —Decide on the name.
    —Decide on the courses.
    —Decide on the vacation schedule.

Topic B: Choose a car for your class, i.e., a car that the class would buy and classmates could borrow.

Topic C: Decide on three ideas for improvements in your town that you would recommend to your mayor.

Topic D: Choose a place for a one-week class trip. You have $2,000 for each student.

Step 4. Have a formal meeting to make recommendations for the topic that your group has chosen. One member should write down your recommendations.

Step 5. After each group has decided on its recommendations, form one group with the whole class. Report your decisions to the whole class.

Agenda

Opening the meeting by the chair.

Reading of the minutes of the last meeting.

Old business.

New business.

Other business.

Setting the date for the next meeting.

Adjournment.

—— ◇ For Fun: Find the ◇ ——
Strange Word

See the teacher's introduction on page 118.

Introductory Exercise

Choose the correct word or phrase and fill in the blanks.

GAME ONE

country   turn   go   right
Germany   months

1. A: Listen to these words. Then tell me which one is strange.

2. B: OK, _____ ahead.

3. A: June, Germany, July, January.

4. B: Oh, I know. _____ is strange.

5. A: Why is it strange?

6. B: Because it's a _____ .

   The others are _____ .

7. A: That's _____ .

   Now it's your _____ .

GAME TWO

Sure   "Plate"   pick up   see   right
Please repeat   Why   got it

8. B: Plate, fork, spoon, cup

9. A: Ummm. Let me _____ . Did you say, "Plate, fork,

knife . . . ?" _____ it, OK?

10. B: _____ . Plate, fork, spoon, cup.

11. A: Oh, I've _____ . _____ doesn't belong.

12. B: _____ ?

13. A: Because we _____ a fork, spoon, and cup
when we eat, but we don't a plate.

14. B: Yes, you're _____ .

GAME THREE

islands   Why   Japan   Sorry   right   Italian
English-speaking country   others   did you say   again

15. A: Next, New Zealand, Switzerland, Japan, Ireland.

16. B: _____ . What _____ ?

Please say it _____ , slowly.

17. A: New Zealand, Switzerland, Japan, Ireland.

18. B: Hmmm. I'm not sure. Japan?

19. A: _____ ?

20. B: The _____ are English-speaking countries?

21. A: No, I don't think Switzerland is an _____ .

They speak French, German, and _____ in Switzerland.

22. B: Oh, I know. Switzerland is different because the others are _____ .
Switzerland isn't.

23. A: Yes, you're _____ . There's also another one.

24. B: I don't know. What?

25. A: _____ isn't like the others because all the
others have "land" in their names.

26. B: Oh, yeah.

Student A

Step 1. Circle the strange word in each group in the list below.

Step 2. Read the list to your partners. They will say which word is strange and why.
Listen to your partners' lists and say which word is strange and why.

1. elephant, lion, dog, fish
4. nose, mouse, eye, leg
7. German, Japan, French, American
10. John, Sue, Tom, Bob
13. tell, talk, hear, speak
16. tennis, basketball, ping-pong, golf
19. 15 minutes after 3, a quarter after 3, 3:50, 15 minutes past 3
22. his, she, my, your
25. cereal, soup, sandwich, steak
28. blue, green, yellow, fight

Step 3. With your partners, write some lists of words in the space below.
Three words should be similar and one strange.

Step 4. Leave your partners and make new groups of 3 or 4 students.
Take turns reading your lists, telling which words are strange, and telling why they are strange.

Student B

Step 1. Circle the strange word in each group in the list below.

Step 2. Read the list to your partners. They will say which word is strange and why.
Listen to your partners' lists and say which word is strange and why.

2. mountain, river, sea, ocean
5. wine, whiskey, water, beer
8. doctor, dentist, nurse, farmer
11. a quarter to two, 1:45, fifteen past two, fifteen minutes to two
14. tiger, chicken, children, lion
17. grandmother, daughter, son, mother
20. policeman, fisherman, Englishman, teacher
23. think, thick, see, thin
26. baseball, bowling, volleyball, basketball
29. train, plane, bus, car

Step 3. With your partners, write some lists of words in the space below. Three words should be similar and one strange.

Step 4. Leave your partners and make new groups of 3 or 4 students. Take turns reading your lists, telling which words are strange, and telling why they are strange.

Student C

Step 1. Circle the strange word in each group in the list below.

Step 2. Read the list to your partners. They will say which word is strange and why.

Listen to your partners' lists and say which word is strange and why.

---

3. paper, pen, book, pencil
6. hats, shoes, boots, socks
9. noon, 5:30, half-past six, thirty minutes after nine
12. August, September, October, November
15. second, fifth, fourth, three
18. see, gave, went, took
21. cookie, lemon, pie, candy
24. light, long, read, lay
27. New York, Mexico, Miami, Moscow
30. apple, banana, salad, orange

Step 3. With your partners, write some lists of words in the space below. Three words should be similar and one strange.

Step 4. Leave your partners and make new groups of 3 or 4 students. Take turns reading your lists, telling which words are strange, and telling why they are strange.

Appendix

General Procedure for All Activities

1. Read or paraphrase the appropriate Teacher's Introduction to the students. This explains the purpose of the activity.

2. Go over the key expressions given in the box on the first page of the activity. Review their meaning and pronunciation.

3. Have the students do the Introductory Exercise. It has two steps:

   a) Individually, the students fill in the blanks.

   b) In pairs, they read their answers to each other.

   You can circulate to answer questions and check the students' answers.

4. The students do the pair/group practice. It may be helpful or even necessary to have two or three students model the first interaction in Step One as an example to be sure everybody understands how to do the practice. As they continue the practice, you can circulate to encourage the use of the key expressions.

Teacher's Introductions for the Activities

Activity 1: Rejoinders

Conversation strategies: Active listening, sustaining the conversation.

Teacher's introduction: Rejoinders are used to show that you are listening, that you understand and that you are interested. If I say, "My dog died last night," and you say nothing, I won't know if you heard me, or I might think you weren't interested. However, if you say, "That's great!" then I know you heard me, but you didn't understand. On the other hand, if you say, "I'm sorry to hear that," then I know you understood me and you were interested in what I said.

Note: Activity 2 also practices rejoinders, but they can be used in almost every activity. Encourage the students to use them throughout these activities.

Activity 2: Follow-up Questions

Conversation strategies: Sustaining the conversation, soliciting others' opinions.

Teacher's introduction: We use follow-up questions to talk more deeply about a topic. If you ask someone a question and they answer it, it is often good to *ask a question about their answer*. Also, by doing this, it shows that you are listening and are interested in what others are saying. In this activity you should also continue to practice rejoinders. So first, let's review some rejoinders.

Activity 3: Confirmation Questions

Conversation strategies: Active listening, confirmation checks, comprehension checks, repairing breakdowns.

Teacher's introduction: Describing the drawings in this activity to each other gives you practice in understanding others and shows you how well you are understood *by* others. If you don't understand your partner because of grammar, vocabulary or pronunciation problems, you need to ask questions to clear up the misunderstanding. This activity will give you practice in asking many different types of questions to help understand your partner.

Activity 4: Clarifications with Question Words

Conversation strategies: Confirmation checks, repairing breakdowns.

Teacher's introduction: If I say to you, "My cousin gave me a jigsaw puzzle," and you say, "Pardon?" I'll know you didn't understand. But I won't know which *word* you didn't understand. It will help me if you let me know specifically which word you didn't understand, so you might ask, "Your cousin gave you a *what?*" Then I know you didn't understand "jigsaw puzzle." Or you might ask, "*Who* gave you a puzzle?" Then I know you didn't understand that I had said "my cousin." This unit will give you practice in asking questions about specific information which you did not understand. And remember to put extra stress on the words in italics for emphasis.

Activity 5: Keeping or Killing the Conversation

Conversation strategies: Sustaining the conversation, soliciting others' opinions, ending the conversation, changing the topic.

Teacher's introduction: Sometimes you are asked a question that you can't or don't want to answer. For example, if I ask you, "What are you going to do this weekend?" and you say, "I don't know," you have *killed the conversation*. To keep the conversation going, you could say, "I'm not sure. What are *you* going to do this weekend?" In this activity, we will practice a technique and some expressions you can use to keep a conversation going, even if someone asks you a difficult question or an embarrassing question. Sometimes you may want to end the conversation or change the topic. Some of the phrases in this lesson can be used to end or change a conversation.

Activity 6: Expressing Probability

Conversation strategies: Preventing breakdowns, expressing probability accurately.

Teacher's introduction: I had a friend who always said "maybe" when I asked her about her plans. Once I asked her if she was coming to my party that weekend. She said, "Maybe I will." Because she said "maybe," I wasn't sure whether to expect her or not. It would have helped me if she had said, "I probably will," or "I doubt it." In this activity, we'll practice expressions to help you speak more specifically about your plans.

Activity 7: Interrupting Someone

Conversation strategies: Clarification requests, interrupting appropriately.

Teacher's introduction: We know it's important to ask questions and to make comments in discussions. However, sometimes when you are part of a big discussion group, it is difficult to stop the conversation to ask a question or make a comment. In this activity, we'll practice expressions you can use in order to *politely* and *naturally* interrupt someone in order to speak.

Note: This activity requires three participants. It could be confusing. It would be a good idea to have three students model interaction # 1 to show how this activity is done.

Activity 8: Echoing Instructions

Conversation strategies: Preventing and repairing breakdowns in communication, confirmation checks, comprehension checks, clarification requests, rephrasing statements.

Teacher's introduction: In this activity we'll practice giving and understanding instructions. Also, we'll practice using some very important expressions to let our partners know that we understand or don't understand what they said. These expressions are, for example, "I've got it," or "Could you repeat that?" They are useful in many situations, not only when giving or getting instructions.

Activity 9: Polite Requests, Responses, and Excuses

Conversation strategies: Requesting and responding appropriately, escaping from a conversation.

Teacher's introduction: All languages have special expressions to show politeness. English does, too. Polite expressions are important for two reasons. First, if you use polite English, you make a good impression on other people. There is research which found that educated and professional people use more polite language. Also, if you need help, for example, and if you can ask another person to help you *politely*, there's a greater chance that the person will say, "OK," and help you. If you are not polite, it is easier for them to say, "No, I'm too busy." Sometimes you may need to say "no" to a request, but you can soften a "no" with an excuse that won't sound impolite. We'll practice some excuses in this activity.

Activity 10: Getting a Response

Conversation strategies: Sustaining the conversation, including others, soliciting others' opinions, comprehension checks.

Teacher's introduction: In this activity we will practice expressions you can use in order to try to include others in a conversation. You can use these expressions to encourage others to give their opinion, to find out if they agree with you, and to find out if they understood your ideas.

Activity 11: Soliciting Details

Conversation strategies: Sustaining the conversation, clarification requests, reflective listening.

Teacher's introduction: In this activity, we will practice expressions you can use in order to get a deeper understanding of what someone has said. If you are not sure you understand someone's ideas, you can use these expressions to ask them to explain in greater detail or with specific examples.

Activity 12: Making Comparisons

Conversation strategies: Confirmation checks, comprehension checks, preventing and repairing breakdowns in communication, clarification requests.

Teacher's introduction: In this activity, you will describe a picture to a partner. This is a good activity to practice using some useful expressions to let someone know you don't understand, to let someone know you *do* understand, or to ask for more information. You will also find out how well you are understood by others. These expressions will be helpful for you anytime you are having a conversation, but you are having difficulty understanding. You will also practice words and expressions that are necessary when two people are comparing something together.

Activity 13: Finding the Right Word

Conversation strategies: Preventing and repairing breakdowns in communication, paraphrasing, and rephrasing.

Teacher's introduction: A learner of English once went into a store but couldn't find what he was looking for. Also he didn't know what it was called in English. The store clerk asked the student to describe it. The student said, "It's a type of fruit. It's long and yellow. We eat the inside, so we must open it first." Do you know what it was? In this activity we will practice the technique of describing words. This is a useful technique to use when we don't know the English word for something or when someone doesn't understand the word we use.

Activity 14: Exploring a Word

Conversation strategies: Clarification requests.

Teacher's introduction: I once said to a student, "That movie was stupendous," and the student said, "What?" I didn't know if the student didn't understand my whole sentence or just a word, or if he couldn't even hear me. So I repeated the sentence louder. Later, I found out he didn't understand "stupendous." If you don't understand a word during a conversation, it's helpful if you ask for specific information about the word; don't just say "What?" For example, you could ask how to spell it, or ask for a synonym or antonym. This is helpful to other people, and it is a good way to learn new vocabulary.

Activity 15: Correcting Someone

Conversation strategies: Clarification requests, correcting appropriately.

Teacher's introduction: Sometimes in a conversation, the person you are talking to might say something that isn't true. Perhaps it was just a mistake. For example, your teacher might say on Friday, "Please give me your essay tomorrow." Actually, she meant Monday or the next school day. Sometimes people say something that they don't know is incorrect, for example, "Chicago is the second largest city in the U.S." If you want to correct someone, it's important that you use polite expressions. In this activity, we will practice these types of expressions.

Activity 16: Eliciting Confirmation

Conversation strategies: Confirmation checks, comprehension checks, preventing and repairing breakdowns in communication, clarification requests.

Teacher's introduction: In this activity we will practice describing furniture in a room. This is good practice for furniture vocabulary and for space vocabulary, for example, "in front of," "in the corner," and "next to." This is also especially good practice for trying to understand your partner and to see if you can be understood. We will practice common expressions like, "Do you see it?" "Can you repeat that?" "Have you got it?" and "I see." These are good expressions, not only for this activity, but also for other conversations. First we need to fill in the vocabulary on page 61.

Activity 17: Starting and Stopping a Conversation

Conversation strategies: Initiating a conversation, sustaining the conversation, ending the conversation.

Teacher's introduction: Many students say that they would like to meet more native English speakers, but they think English speakers are not open to talking to them. If you want to meet someone new, often *you* must start the conversation. In this activity, we will practice techniques you can use to start conversations with someone you don't know. Also, we'll practice some polite and natural techniques you can use to find out if—and when—your conversation partner is ready to *end* the conversation.

Activity 18: Beginning and Ending a Phone Call

Conversation strategies: Using telephone conversation conventions, soliciting information.

Teacher's introduction: Many students have said that it is difficult to talk on the phone in English. It seems especially difficult to know what to say *first* and how to *end* the phone conversation. In this activity, we will practice natural and polite expressions that are commonly used when we talk on the phone.

Activity 19: Expressing Opinions

Conversation strategies: Sustaining the conversation, expressing agreement and disagreement.

Teacher's introduction: In American culture, it's OK to give your opinion and to disagree with another person's opinion. But if you give your opinion or you disagree with that person, it's important that you be polite. If a beginning-level student disagrees with another person's opinion, they will probably just say, "No!" or "You're wrong." These expressions are not very polite. If a student is more advanced, they will probably use a more polite expression, like, "I'm afraid I disagree." In this activity, we will practice polite expressions for giving our opinion, for disagreeing and for agreeing.

Activity 20: Making a Group Decision

Conversation strategies: Sustaining the conversation, expressing opinions, soliciting others' opinions.

Teacher's introduction: In this activity, you will practice expressions that you can use when you are trying to make a decision with someone. For example, you might be planning what to do on the weekend with some friends. It's important that you not only make some suggestions, but also give your opinion about their suggestions. This is what you'll practice in this activity.

Note: This activity requires groups of 3-4 people.

Activity 21: Discussion Connectors

Conversation strategies: Confirmation checks, comprehension checks, preventing and repairing breakdowns in communication, clarification requests, sustaining the conversation.

Teacher's introduction: In this activity you will lead a discussion and take part in a discussion with two or three other students. We want to have an active discussion, not a passive discussion. For example, in a *passive* discussion, the leader asks a question. One person answers the question. Then the leader asks a second question. The second person answers, etc. This is not a good or active discussion. In an active discussion, the leader poses a question to all the members. One member answers and perhaps a second member asks a follow-up question. Perhaps a member asks for the leader's opinion or asks the leader to explain something. In an active discussion, all members give their opinions, ask questions, ask follow-up questions, and use rejoinders. The leader just starts the discussion.

Note: This activity requires groups of at least three. It uses many of the conversation strategies and is a good review. It could be repeated from time to time.

Activity 22: Summarizing

Conversation strategies: Active listening, preventing breakdowns, confirmation checks, paraphrasing, understanding responses, summarizing.

Teacher's introduction: In a conversation, it is often helpful if you can let the other person know that you are listening, that you are interested, and that you understand. A good way to do this is to summarize in one sentence the main idea that the other person is expressing. If your summary is wrong, the other person can explain more and help you understand. In this activity, we will practice some useful expressions to summarize what someone says to us.

Activity 23: Formal Meetings

Conversation strategies: Following the conventions of a formal meeting.

Teacher's introduction: As you are now at a high level of conversation ability, you may have a chance to join some clubs or join a company in which meetings take place in English. There are certain steps which we follow during a meeting and there are special expressions we use during meetings. For example, in a meeting, if we want to make a suggestion, we don't say, "I *think we should* buy a video." Instead, we say, "I *move* we buy a video." In this activity, we will practice having a meeting. We will use the special expressions and follow the special rules of a formal meeting.

Note: This activity requires groups of 4-5 students.

Activity 24: Find the Strange Word

Conversation strategies: Confirmation checks, clarification requests.

Teacher's introduction: This activity is a little different. It's for fun, like a word game. I will say four words to you and you tell me which is strange: Monday, Tuesday, November, Friday. Which word is strange? Why? In this activity, you will read lists of words and tell which words are strange and why. This will be a good challenge for your pronunciation, listening, and speaking. This is also good practice for asking someone to repeat something and for telling them that they are right.

Note: This activity is somewhat different from the others in that its format is not typical of everyday conversation patterns. It's a classroom game. However, the students do practice useful strategies as they play the game.

This activity is played with 3-4 students.

On Strategic Competence

The communicative approach seems to be well-established now in the profession of language teaching. It's a hard one to argue against since, after all, the purpose of language learning and language itself does seem to be communication. Language is the medium, not the message. At the same time, the notion of competence has become attached to the term "communication" to suggest that there are identifiable abilities and skills that communicators need to master. It's easy to see that linguistic competence is one area of competency: Learners need to pronounce well, follow grammatical rules, and learn a lot of words. We also know that as learners become proficient in the basic linguistic skills, they also need to develop competence in the socio-linguistic dimension of language use so that they communicate in culturally and socially appropriate ways. Contemporary teaching materials do try to help the learners develop these competencies.

In recent years, another dimension of communicative competence has become recognized and labeled—strategic competence. It is an area that still lacks the precise definition of a formal grammar or a functional syllabus or even a sociolinguistic description of social levels of language use. However, it does seem to be a competency area that needs to be learned and taught. There are words, phrases, and conventions that are used as two speakers engage in the active give-and-take of communicating through conversation. Some features of this competency area may be common from one language to another, but some may be different, and the difference can interfere with the success of a language user. For example, we all make mistakes or grope for a word as we use language, even our native language, but there are effective and ineffective ways of repairing a faulty utterance or paraphrasing a missing lexical item. Learners need awareness of and practice in these strategic competencies.

We at Pro Lingua Associates have not seen many materials that feature conversation practice and also bring strategic competencies to the learner's attention. So, when David and Peggy Kehe sent us their manuscript, it caught our eye because that seemed to be what their conversation activities were doing. They had developed a series of pair and group activities for use in Japan to help students become better at conversational fluency. But more than that, their activities addressed the area of strategic competency in English.

We are pleased to have found this delightful and very useful book, and we think you will find that these activities will bring a new dimension into your language classes and programs.

RCC for Pro Lingua Associates

Index to Conversation Strategies

Numbers indicate activity number.

ELICITING CONFIRMATION